TRAVELLERS

SRI LANKA

By
ANDREW FORBES

Written by Andrew Forbes, updated by Katerina Roberts
Original photography by CPA Media

Published by Thomas Cook Publishing
A division of Thomas Cook Tour Operations Limited.
Company registration no. 3772199 England
The Thomas Cook Business Park, Unit 9, Coningsby Road,
Peterborough PE3 8SB, United Kingdom
E-mail: books@thomascook.com, Tel: + 44 (0) 1733 416477
www.thomascookpublishing.com

Produced by Cambridge Publishing Management Limited
Burr Elm Court, Main Street, Caldecote CB23 7NU

ISBN: 978-1-84848-155-8

© 2005, 2007 Thomas Cook Publishing
This third edition © 2009
Text © Thomas Cook Publishing
Maps © Thomas Cook Publishing

Series Editor: Maisie Fitzpatrick
Production/DTP: Steven Collins

Printed and bound in Italy by Printer Trento

Cover photography: Front L–R: all © Thomas Cook.
Back: © Andy Rouse/Getty

Contents

KEY TO MAPS

✈ Airport   ★ Start of walk/tour

▲
320m Mountain   ■ Public building

∩ Ancient walls   ＼ Railway line

Introduction

Perhaps the most beautiful country in South Asia, Sri Lanka has an appeal which has drawn visitors over the centuries, first for its rich spice and gem markets, and more recently for its pristine beaches and magnificent hill country. It's also a cultural treasure trove, with historic sites stretching back over two thousand years.

Over the millennia, Sri Lanka has been known by a plethora of names. In the ancient Hindu epic *Ramayana*, the island is referred to as Lanka or Sri Lanka. The meaning of Lanka is doubtful; it may translate as 'shining' or 'resplendent'. Sri is a common prefix to names or titles and means 'noble'. Thus, Sri Lanka means 'Noble and Resplendent'. The first Sinhalese on the island (*see p10*) called it Tabbapanni, or 'Copper Coloured', a name corrupted by the Greeks and Romans to Taprobane.

In due time, the island's inhabitants set out to bestow a more heroic name on their country and called it Sinhala-Dvipa or 'Lion Island'. The Sinhala part in the name was later corrupted into Selan, Ceilao, and thence to Ceylon. Certainly the latter was adopted by the British, and remained the official name of the country until 24 years after independence. In 1972 it reverted to its ancient name of Sri Lanka. Today the full official name of the country is Sri Lanka Prajatantrika Samajavadi Janarajya, or the 'Democratic Socialist Republic of Sri Lanka'.

Whatever designation it goes by, Sri Lanka is – or should be – synonymous with the archetypal paradise island. For such a relatively small place, there's an amazing amount to see and do.

THE 2004 TSUNAMI

On 26 December 2004, coastal areas of eastern and southern Sri Lanka were devastated by the Indian Ocean tsunami, causing immense structural damage and loss of life in the areas that it hit. Fortunately, in most places the damage extended no more than a few hundred metres inland.

Following huge injections of foreign aid and ongoing self-help projects, Sri Lanka is showing positive signs of recovery. Work by non-governmental agencies has made a difference to many people's lives with new housing developments, schools, community centres and a greatly improved infrastructure. Many regions have returned to normality with hotels rebuilt or refurbished to international standards, and tourism, upon which so much of the economy depends, is destined to bring many visitors back to this friendly island.

There's a broad range of ethnic, cultural and religious diversity to delight and stimulate the mind, and the gastronomic offerings available across the island are mouth-wateringly delicious. Add this to the pristine white sand beaches, warm blue seas and the wide variety of water sports on offer, and it's apparent that there is no question of the visitor getting bored. What's more, it's relatively inexpensive and really good value for money by international standards.

Introduction

Unawatuna, a secluded beach near Galle

The land

Sri Lanka is an island located at 7° 0' north in latitude and 80° 0' east in longitude. Over the centuries its shape has reminded mapmakers and travellers of a teardrop, or sometimes of a pearl.

The shortest distance to India, from Point Pedro in the north of the island across the Palk Straits, is a mere 48km (30 miles), and there are indications that once upon a time there was a land connection between the two countries via **Adam's Bridge** (*see p140*). With an area of 65,610sq km (25,332sq miles), Sri Lanka is a little less than the size of The Netherlands and Belgium combined. Sri Lanka has a coastline almost 1,600km (1,000 miles) long, and this is one of the country's major attractions and sources of wealth.

Hardly less beautiful is the immensely fertile hill country, located in the central southern region. It was once covered with dense jungles, but vast tracts of forest were cut down in the 19th and 20th centuries to make way for coffee, tea, palm and rubber plantations.

Rice is the people's staple food, and the major crop of the island, but coconuts are tremendously important too (*see pp26–7*). Known down the centuries for its wealth in spices (*see pp48–9*), the island is also famed for its extensive tea estates (*see pp8–9*) and for

Madampe paddy fields

The beautiful central hill country

the gem industry, centred on Ratnapura, the 'City of Jewels'. In the central hill regions, near the former colonial health resort of Nuwara Eliya, Sri Lanka's highest mountain, at 2,524m (8,281ft), is Pidurutalagala. Though rather lower, the most famous and revered mountain in the country is **Adam's Peak**, locally known as Sri Pada or 'Noble Footprint', an important pilgrimage site for all the island's major religions.

Due to regionally uneven precipitation, Sri Lanka is geographically divided into a wet zone and a dry zone. The latter makes up around three-quarters of the country. The wet zone comprises the southwestern region and the western, central and southern hill areas. The dry zone encompasses the southeast, east and north of the island. The term 'dry' is relative, though, since rainfall during the monsoon season is still heavy, but not as immense as in the wet zone. Sri Lanka has two separate monsoon

seasons, one from May to November which affects the western and southern regions (the southwest monsoon), the other from November to January, which affects the northeastern and eastern regions (the northeast monsoon). This means that the best time to visit the popular southwestern beaches is between November and February, conveniently just in the middle of the northern hemisphere's winter. Visitors should bear in mind that although set firmly in the tropics and not far from the equator, the hill country can get quite chilly at night, while the wild and windswept Horton Plains can be downright cold, especially between November and February. There are a few offshore islands, especially in the north near Jaffna, but south of the island the immensity of the Indian Ocean, broken only by a few tiny coral islets, stretches all the way to Antarctica.

Tea

Tea was first introduced to Europe from China by the Portuguese in the early 16th century. In 1667, the British East India Company ordered its first shipment of tea from China. It arrived two years later. Soon it became Britain's favourite drink. In the 1830s the East India Company began growing tea on an experimental basis in Assam in India. In 1840, the first hundred boxes of Assam tea reached Britain. At about the same time, 200 tea seedlings were brought from Assam to Ceylon and planted there.

In 1849 a Scot, James Taylor, started the first commercial tea plantation in Ceylon. This was highly fortuitous, as the devastating 'coffee plague' which took hold in 1868 destroyed most of the island's coffee crop, after which the cultivation of coffee was discontinued and replaced with tea.

Tea is made from the leaves of the tea plant, *Camellia sinensis*. This tree can grow to a height of 10m (33ft), but to facilitate the harvesting of the leaves it is regularly trimmed to the size of a shrub. The shrubs are usually kept at a height of 0.8–1.5m (2^1/$_2$–5ft). Every 3–4 years they are cut even lower, which extends their life span. Some of today's shrubs are said to hail back to the pioneering days of tea cultivation in Sri Lanka –

The freshly picked leaves of the tea plant

In a more coarse picking method, whole branches are picked clean of their leaves and buds, resulting in a poorer product. Depending on the location of the tea plantation, the leaves are picked every one to four weeks – the higher the location of the plantation, the less the frequency. Having collected the leaves in the baskets on their backs, the tea pickers carry them to the factory. There, the leaves are first dried in the open air; this takes 16–24 hours. Then they are rolled and crushed, which initiates the fermentation of the tannin in the leaves. To complete the fermentation, the leaves are spread out on drying racks, which are located in a well-aired, humid and cool room. There the leaves are left for about 1–2 hours. Finally, the leaves will be dried in a special oven, then sieved and packed.

Depending on the quality of the leaves used, the tea is marked with different grades:

1 **Broken Orange Pekoe:** small leaves with buds.

2 **Broken Pekoe:** medium leaves without buds.

3 **Pekoe:** large, black and twisted leaves.

4 **Pekoe Souchong:** very strong black leaves.

5 **Fannings:** small and grainy leaves.

6 **Dust:** fine tea powder.

Tea plantation workers

which would make them around 130 years old!

The first usable tea leaves are produced sometime between the third and seventh year in the life of the plant. The best tea is the so-called highland tea; it is grown 1,400–2,300m (4,600–7,500ft) above sea level, where sunny days follow cold nights and in between there is frequent fog. The flavour also depends on the speed of growth – the slower the growth, the better the flavour. As a rule, growth is slower in the higher regions.

According to experts, 'two leaves and a bud' is the magical formula for picking tea. Such delicately picked tea is said to be of the highest quality.

History

As with every ancient nation, the early history of Sri Lanka is lost in the mists of time. The earliest inhabitants that we know of – and that does not necessarily mean they were the first inhabitants – are the aboriginal Vedda (see p25), who may have lived on the island for several thousand years.

Some time around 500 BC an Indo-European people, the Sinhalese, arrived on the island and began its settlement and the gradual usurpation of Vedda land. According to the great Sri Lankan epic the *Mahavansa*, these settlers were the followers of Prince Vijaya, who had been expelled from his father's kingdom somewhere in northern India for misconduct. Be that as it may, historians are inclined to agree that the original Sinhalese settlers sailed to Sri Lanka from somewhere in the Gujarat region, perhaps near the mouth of the Indus, and landed somewhere on the west coast of the island, perhaps near Negombo.

Gradually the Sinhalese settlers moved inland, making their first capital at Upatissa, a site that has yet to be identified. In 437 BC King Pandukabhaya founded Anuradhapura, and this would become the major seat of Sinhalese power for well over 1,000 years.

Approximately two centuries later, around 249 BC, King Tissa of Anuradhapura was converted to Buddhism (*see p30*), another immensely important milestone in the history of Sri Lanka. The new religion was gradually adopted by virtually the entire Sinhalese population, until being Buddhist became virtually synonymous with being Sinhalese. Buddhism and the state also became closely intertwined, so that it soon effectively became the national religion.

Then, in 205 BC, the first recorded Tamil invasion from southern India occurred. The Tamil Cholas seized Anuradhapura and began the long history of Sinhalese–Tamil rivalry and hostility which continues to the present day. The Tamils were South Indian Dravidians, not North Indian Aryans, and they were Hindu, not Buddhist.

There began a titanic struggle between the Tamils and the Sinhalese which lasted for over 1,000 years. First one side then the other would seize the advantage. Anuradhapura was captured and recaptured, looted and rebuilt until, in the 11th century, the Sinhalese moved their capital to Polonnaruwa in a bid to avoid Tamil attacks. Yet this was to no avail – Polonnaruwa reached its zenith in 1187–96 under the redoubtable King Nissanka Malla, but by the early 13th century renewed warfare with the Tamils had resulted in its looting and partial destruction, and it was abandoned as a capital in 1293.

Up to the late 16th century, the capital moved many times. First it was threatened just by Tamil invaders, but in 1498 the Portuguese appeared in Indian waters. The capitals came and went, often in rivalry with one another: Dambadeniya, Yapahuwa, Panduwas

Nuwara, Kurunegala, Gampola, Kotte and Sitawaka (near today's Avissawella). Kotte lasted longest (1371–1565), whereas Sitawaka (1521–94) was sacked at least five times during its short existence. Sitawaka's final destruction came at the hands of the Portuguese, against whom it had put up fierce resistance. Sitawaka's legacy of defiance in the face of European colonial power was now left to the Kingdom of Kandy, which lay sheltered in the mountains of the interior.

In 1505, a Portuguese fleet under the command of Lorenzo d'Almeida arrived in Colombo. The Portuguese established friendly relations with the kingdom of Kotte, which ruled over the

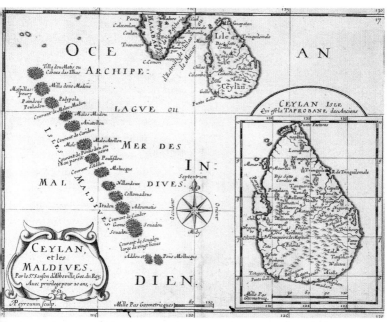

French map of Ceylon and the Maldives, dated 1652

area around Colombo. Only 12 years later, having become aware of the potential of the spice trade, most of all cinnamon, did the Portuguese begin to pursue commercial aims. They sought permission to build a fortified trading post, which was granted. Their first trading settlement near Colombo aroused protests from the local populace, particularly the Muslim traders, who did not take kindly to competition; the settlement had to be abandoned. Still, the Portuguese continued their drive to take control of the cinnamon trade, and they established a fort at Colombo.

In the mid-17th century, the Portuguese laid siege to the harbours of Batticaloa and Trincomalee, which were part of the kingdom of Kandy. King

The last king of Kandy in a wall painting, Asgiriya Vihara, Kandy

Rajasinha II (1635–87) sought assistance from the Dutch, who had entered the scene in 1602, when Admiral Spilbergen had anchored near Batticaloa. The Dutch also sought control of the lucrative cinnamon trade, which they planned to wrest from the Portuguese.

After negotiations, the king of Kandy gained the assistance of the Dutch against the Portuguese. But the price was high: as part of their agreement the Kandyans had to pay the Dutch for their military intervention, and in case of non-payment, it was stipulated, the Dutch would hold on to the lowlands which they had but recently occupied. The Dutch succeeded in expelling the Portuguese in 1658. Immediately afterwards, they presented their bill to the Kandyan king – a sum they knew would be far beyond Rajasinha's means. The Dutch stratagem worked and they became masters over the lowlands, a large part of Sri Lanka.

As with the Portuguese, Dutch rule on the island was limited to about one and a half centuries. In the wake of the European wars of the 18th century, the Dutch were forced to cede their fleet to the British and also had to hand over their Sri Lankan territories. In August 1795, British troops marched towards the fort of Trincomalee to take possession. After some considerable resistance, the Dutch finally hoisted the white flag. In February 1796, British ships landed at Colombo and Negombo, which offered only token resistance. Not content with the lowlands alone, in the following two decades the British turned their attention towards Kandy, which to that time had never been conquered. In 1815 Kandy was taken and the British became undisputed rulers of the whole island.

British rule lasted for 150 years and was, by and large, fairly enlightened. The British were more interested in trade and maintaining a Pax Britannica across South Asia than in religious conversion. Nevertheless, Sri Lankan nationalism, both Sinhalese and Tamil, continued to grow, and by 1948, the same year in which India and Pakistan gained their independence, Sri Lanka became a free nation through an agreed peaceful transfer of power.

Unfortunately, subsequent years saw a resurgence of Sinhalese–Tamil rivalries which split the island. This was compounded in 1949 when almost a million 'Indian Tamils' were declared stateless, and again in 1956 when Sinhalese was made the national language.

The first communal clashes between the two groups began in 1958. Subsequently vicious massacres, mainly of Tamils, occurred in 1983, and a destructive civil war that would plague the island for nearly two decades broke out. By 2001 it had become apparent that neither side could win an outright victory. The island's economy was on the verge of bankruptcy, the people war-weary, and a compromise seemed the only way out. In 2002 a ceasefire brought temporary peace, but by 2008 this was broken following increasing ethnic tension and several bomb attacks in Colombo (*see pp142–3*).

ntrance to the Dutch ramparts at Matara, dated 1780

The Cloud Maidens of Sigiriya

'Sweet girl, standing on the mountain, your teeth are like jewels, lighting the lotus of your eyes. Talk to me gently of your heart…
Who is not happy when he sees those rosy palms, rounded shoulders, gold necklaces, copper-hued lips and long, long eyes'

Graffito, *Sigiriya Mirror Wall*, c. AD 800

The famous Sigiriya frescoes found in central Sri Lanka, painted in tempera on the rock face, date from around the time of Kasyapa (*see pp120–21*). Exquisitely painted in brilliant colours, they are strongly reminiscent of contemporaneous Gupta cave paintings at Ajanta near Bombay. They are apparently secular in character, and having no obvious religious significance are generally considered to be representations of the beauties in Kasyapa's court. An inscription on the nearby Mirror Wall speaks of 'Five Hundred Golden Ones', but at the time of their rediscovery only 22 survived. Some, loosely designated *viju-lata* or 'lightning princesses', are light-skinned, whilst others, known as *megha-lata* or 'cloud maidens', are of darker hue.

The forms of these celestial maidens rise above delicate clouds at waist level. They are elaborately bejewelled and their ample breasts are barely concealed by diaphanous gauze garments. Some hold flowers or trays of flowers in their hands. They are extremely sensuous – a quality readily noticed that has aroused conflicting emotions in visitors to Sigiriya down the years. Thus, a male admirer incising his thoughts on the Mirror Wall

'A deer-eyed maiden'

1,000 years ago was so moved that he wrote:

'The ladies who wear golden chains on their breasts beckon to me. Now I have seen these resplendent ladies, heaven has lost its appeal for me.'

A contemporary female, clearly less enamoured with the frescoes, has left a record of different, if equally passionate, emotions:

'A deer-eyed maiden of the mountain side arouses anger in my mind. In her hand she holds a string of pearls, and in her eyes she assumes rivalry with me.'

This worldly sensuality may explain early damage to the Sigiriya nymphs, for it is speculated that disapproving Buddhist monks may have destroyed those frescoes within reach centuries ago. Certainly misplaced Puritanism seems the most likely explanation of a vicious night attack during October 1967, when all but one of the surviving frescoes were daubed and disfigured with paint by persons unknown. So serious was the damage that specialists had to be called in from Italy to restore the frescoes, which are now officially recognised as a national treasure and protected as a part of a UNESCO World Heritage Site.

Unfortunately, during the attack three of the maidens were damaged beyond repair, so security at the

Sigiriya Cloud Maidens

site is pretty tight today. Flash photography is forbidden, and guards are permanently on hand to keep an eye on visitors. It's quite a climb to the Mirror Wall, and an ascent of the vertigo-inducing spiral staircase, completely clad in rusting steel mesh and now in serious need of restoration or replacement, is not for the faint-hearted. The reward is well worth the effort, however – and when at last you stand, catching your breath and marvelling at the cloud maidens, spare a thought for the intrepid artists, clearly inspired by visions of celestial beauty, as they clung to their precarious perch so many centuries ago!

History

c. **500** BC	Sinhalese settlers arrive from North India.
437 BC	Anuradhapura becomes the first capital.
c. **249** BC	King Tissa is converted to Buddhism.
205 BC	First recorded Tamil invasion from South India. More than 1,000 years of intermittent warfare between Sinhalese and Tamils begin.
c. AD **400**	Arab navigators from Yemen and Oman begin to visit Sri Lanka on a regular basis.
1055	The capital is moved to Polonnaruwa.
1505	The Portuguese arrive in Colombo, marking the beginning of European interest in the island.
1658	The Dutch replace the Portuguese; Kandy retains its independence.
1795	The British begin to replace the Dutch as masters of the lowlands.
1815	The British take control of Kandy and become masters of the entire island.

Admiral Spilbergen at the Kandy court (Dutch Museum, Colombo)

1833	English is decreed to be the official language.
1931	The British grant the right to vote and introduce power sharing.
1948	Ceylon gains full independence.
1949	Indian Tamil plantation workers disenfranchised.
1956	Solomon Bandaranaike is elected on a wave of Sinhalese nationalism. Sinhala is made the sole official language.
1959	Bandaranaike assassinated by Buddhist monk.
1960	Ceylon elects the world's first woman PM, Srimavo Bandaranaike.
1965	The opposition United National Party wins elections and attempts to reverse the nationalisation measures.
1970	Srimavo Bandaranaike returns to power and starts to extend the nationalisation programme.
1972	Ceylon changes its name to Sri Lanka and Buddhism is given primary place as the country's religion, further antagonising the Tamil minority.
1976	The Liberation Tigers of Tamil Eelam (LTTE) is formed as tensions increase in Tamil-dominated areas of the north and east.
1983	Anti-Tamil riots lead to the deaths of several hundred Tamils. Conflict develops in the north between army and the LTTE.
1987	Government forces push the LTTE back into northern city of Jaffna.
1990	Violence between Sri Lankan army and separatists escalates.
1991	The LTTE implicated in the assassination of Indian premier Rajiv Gandhi in southern India.
1993	President Premadasa killed in an LTTE bomb attack.
1994	President Kumaratunga comes to power pledging to end war.
1995	Peace talks collapse and the LTTE resumes its bombing

campaign. The government launches a major offensive, driving separatists out of Jaffna.

1996 The state of emergency is extended across the country after the LTTE bombs Colombo.

1998 The Tamil Tigers bomb Sri Lanka's holiest Buddhist site, the Temple of the Tooth in Kandy.

1999 President Kumaratunga is wounded in a bomb attack at an election rally. She is re-elected president.

2000 The LTTE captures strategic Elephant Pass in north of island in April. President Kumaratunga's People's Alliance wins general elections in October.

2001 Britain labels the LTTE as 'terrorists' under new anti-terrorism law designed to halt funding and support for UK-based militant groups. Ranil Wickramasinghe is sworn in as Prime Minister after the opposition United National Party win elections.

2002 Government and Tamil Tiger rebels sign a permanent ceasefire agreement. At peace talks in Norway the government and rebels agree to share power. Tamils to have autonomy in the mainly Tamil north and east.

People's Liberation Front (JVP) Building, Galle

Political poster, Colombo Fort

2004　Early general elections held amid political power struggle. President Kumaratunga wins 105 of 225 parliamentary seats, falling short of overall majority. Mahinda Rajapaksa sworn in as Prime Minister. Split between LTTE Northern Commander Prabakharan and LTTE Eastern Commander Karuna threatens ceasefire.

2004–5　A massive tsunami devastates the coastlines of the Indian Ocean on 26 December 2004. The southern and eastern coasts of Sri Lanka take the full force of the wave, killing thousands and causing widespread damage, although Colombo and inland regions are unaffected. Thanks to prompt international aid and the determination of the Sri Lankan people, reconstruction of the affected areas begins almost immediately.

2006–9　Renewed fighting between government and LTTE results in end of 2002 ceasefire. Ethnic tension and escalating violence in the north and east result in roadside bomb attacks on civilians and ministers.

The vital rubber crop

Rubber trees in the Peak Wilderness area

Christopher Columbus, on his second voyage to the New World at the close of the 15th century, observed Haitian natives playing a game with a ball made from the gum of a tree. Yet rubber – for that was the substance Columbus had seen – only really came to international prominence in the 19th century.

Natural rubber is obtained almost exclusively from the tropical tree *Hevea brasiliensis*, which, as its name suggests, is native to Brazil. In 1876, however, Englishman Sir Henry Wickham collected rubber seeds in the Amazon jungle and took them back to England to plant in Kew Gardens. The young trees were then transplanted to Sri Lanka (as well as to Malaysia) where they thrived, forming the basis of a rubber plantation industry which today produces around three million tons of natural rubber each year.

Most of this natural rubber is still obtained from the trees as it was in the early days. Once the tree is between five and seven years old, the process known as tapping begins. The trunk is scored with a knife, as high up as is practical, to a depth of 1cm ($^1/_3$ inch) and at an angle of thirty degrees left to right. A collection pot is placed at the lower end of the cut, and latex – a milky white fluid – oozes out from between the outer cork and the inner cambium layers of the tree.

The latex thus obtained is sieved to remove impurities, and mixed with water in a coagulation tank. Dilute acid is added and the rubber coagulates on aluminium partitions in the tank. The slabs of rubber are washed and passed through rollers to remove excess water. The rubber is then further treated, in accordance with its intended final use, and baled for shipping.

The practical applications of rubber today are myriad. Aside from footwear, rainwear and tyres – the latter alone accounts for around 70 per cent of consumption – rubber is employed wherever its particular qualities of resilience and strength are valued. Thus we find it serving as conveyor belts and drive belts in factories, as hosing wherever fluids must be moved around, and as cable insulation above and below ground where impermeable seals and a tight fit are essential. Engineers also make

Collecting the latex

heavy use, in the foundations of large buildings and bridges, of rubber's insulating properties against vibration.

It is not just in industry and construction that rubber has found its place, though. The humble rubber band is in use all over the world, as is the eraser, from which rubber got its name. (In 1770, the English chemist Joseph Priestley noted that the substance, which had until then been called 'caoutchouc', could be used to rub out pencil marks and so renamed it 'rubber'.) Finally, in the form of contraceptives, rubber is playing an increasingly vital role in population control and in limiting the spread of AIDS and other STDs.

Ratnapura rubber tapping

People

By the end of the 20th century, Sri Lanka's population was close to 19 million, with perhaps another million, mainly Tamil refugees, living overseas, especially in India and Canada. The largest ethnic group in the island are the mainly Buddhist Sinhalese, who make up around 74 per cent of the population, while the second-largest ethnic group, the Tamils, constitute about 18 per cent.

Neither of the two communities is indigenous to Sri Lanka, though both have shared the island for many, many centuries. Both groups are immigrants from India seeking to promote their claim to the country as a homeland.

Sinhalese and Tamil schoolgirls outside Nuwara Eliya Catholic Church

Long-simmering tensions came to a head in the 1980s, with the Tamils trying to secure equal rights as a minority, and the Sinhalese attempting to strengthen their status as the dominant community.

The tensions between these two principal ethnic groups stem mainly from their different religious and racial backgrounds. The Sinhalese trace their origin to the legendary prince Vijaya, said to have come from North India sometime in the 5th century BC. Vijaya was supposedly banished by his father, King Sinhabahu. The prince set sail with 700 followers, and after their arrival in Sri Lanka they spread over the island, founding the first cities. According to the *Mahavansa*, the most valuable Sri Lankan historical chronicle, Vijaya and his entourage arrived in Sri Lanka on the very day the Buddha died in India. This version of events is plainly an attempt to give credence to the Sinhalese claim to be the preordained guardians of the

Buddhist faith. The Sinhalese were but one of many bands of Aryan descendants who set out to conquer, or at least dominate, the darker-skinned non-Aryan races they encountered during their southward migrations.

Unlike the Sinhalese, the Tamils of Sri Lanka are not an entirely homogeneous ethnic group. Though of the same Dravidian Tamil stock, they are divided into 'Ceylon Tamils' (or 'Jaffna Tamils') and 'Indian Tamils'. The more numerous Ceylon Tamils claim descent from the warrior dynasties which invaded Sri Lanka from the 3rd century BC and which often ruled over large parts of the island; they mainly inhabit the area around Jaffna and the east coast. Indian Tamils, on the other hand, are the descendants of Tamils who were transported to Sri Lanka by the British in the 19th century to work on the tea plantations. Initially, only men made the journey across the Palk Straits, but from the 1880s onwards women and even whole families arrived in Sri Lanka. The floodgates of immigration had opened wide, and by the 1920s half a million Tamils worked in the tea estates. Even today, most Indian Tamils live in the tea-growing areas in the central hills, though a large number have settled in the capital Colombo.

About three-quarters of Tamils are Hindus, the remainder being Christians or Muslims. The language spoken by both groups is also called Tamil, a Dravidian language, which possesses a large number of loan words from Sanskrit. There are hardly any similarities with the Sinhalese language, and as the Indian and the Ceylon Tamils migrated to Sri Lanka during

Muslims chatting in Colombo

Fishermen bringing in their catch in Negombo

historical periods many years apart, they speak widely differing dialects of Tamil. The language uses its own script, which is related to the scripts of the other major Dravidian languages of South India.

At around seven per cent, the third-largest ethnic groups are the Moors, originally descendants of Arab and subsequently Indian merchants who settled in Sri Lanka from the 7th century onwards (*see pp132–3*). Most of them were attracted by the island's status as a centre of commerce, and still today many Moors are businessmen, often in the gem trade. A smaller proportion of the Moors are of Malay extraction. The Malay Moors are concentrated around the south coast town of Hambantota (*see p92*) and are the descendants of Malay seafarers and

soldiers who had been encouraged to settle there by the Dutch. During the British period, regiments of Malay soldiers were stationed in an area called Slave Island in Colombo (*see p50*). Some of the Malays still speak the language of their forefathers, Bahasa Melayu, but the number of speakers is declining rapidly. Otherwise they speak Sinhalese or, in the north and east of the island, Tamil.

A further addition to Sri Lanka's colourful ethnic mosaic are the Burghers, who are of a mixed Sri Lankan–Portuguese or Sri Lankan–Dutch descent. Unlike in India, where mixed European-Indian offspring were despised by British and Indian alike, the Dutch held them in high esteem and the Burghers often rose to high social ranks. The Portuguese for a time even actively encouraged the marriage of their citizens with locals. After independence the mainly English-speaking Burghers lost their influence and many emigrated to Western countries, mostly the USA and Australia. Today, the Burghers make up less than half a per cent of the population. The majority are Christians.

Sri Lanka's forgotten community are the Veddas, erstwhile masters of the island. They are the aboriginals of Sri Lanka, who inhabited the island long before the Sinhalese or the Tamils arrived. Many anthropologists regard them as the direct descendants of Stone Age man, and there seems to be some relationship to the Australian aborigines and the inhabitants of the Andaman Islands. As the population on the island increased and the forests were cut down, the Veddas were gradually forced to give up their traditional way of life. Today, there are only a few hundred of them left, mainly eking out a living as small-time farmers in the jungles of Uva Province.

Finally, Sri Lanka's confusing ethnic mix is completed by tiny minorities of Chinese, Pakistanis, and people of Indian descent such as Parsees, Sindhis and the Islamic Khojas and Bohras.

Decoration at the Temple of the Tooth, Kandy

The coconut palm

'Cocas are the fruits of palm trees, and as we have bread, wine, oil, and vinegar, so ... they extract all these things from this one tree.'

Pigafetta, *Viaggio Intorno il Mondo*, 1519

The coconut palm, or *Cocos nucifera*, is valued not just for its beauty, but also as a lucrative cash crop. Cultivated throughout the South Seas and Indian Ocean regions, it provides food, drink, shelter, transport, fuel, medicine and even clothing for millions of people.

Most of Sri Lanka's coconuts are produced on small plantations. Unhusked ripe nuts are laid on their sides close together in nursery beds

Plaiting coconut palm leaf spines to make a food cover

and almost covered with soil. After 4–10 months the seedlings are transplanted to a field, where they are spaced at distances of 8–10m (9–11yds). Palms usually start bearing fruit after five or six years. Fruits require a year to ripen, and the annual yield per tree may be as high as 100 nuts – though 50 is considered acceptable.

The mature fruits consist of a thick, fibrous husk surrounding the familiar single-seeded nut we see in commerce. The clear liquid within the nut makes a nutritious and refreshing drink, but the real treasure within is the white meat, which is known as copra when dried.

Copra is a rich source of vegetable fat, which can be used in the manufacture of soaps, detergents, shampoos, synthetic rubber and glycerine. After refining to remove fatty acids, it is used in making cooking oils, margarine and cosmetics. Copra products and coconut milk are also widely used in cooking and flavouring, particularly in South and Southeast Asian cuisines.

A bright array of coconuts

But the value of the coconut does not lie in the content of the nut alone. Almost every part of the tree is useful to humans – leading to the saying that there are as many uses for the coconut as there are days of the year.

To begin with, the thin shell of the nut can be carved and manufactured into many useful objects such as spoons, bowls and containers. The thick, fibrous husk, known as coir after processing, is used in making rope, mats, baskets, brushes, brooms, fishing nets, charcoal and even water-resistant clothing.

Mature coconut palms grow to a height of around 25m (80ft), and are surmounted by a graceful crown of giant, feather-like leaves that rustle and crack in the wind. Besides providing shade and a soothing balm to the eye, the coconut trunk – which grows unusually straight – provides excellent wood for fishing vessels, housing and furniture. When treated and polished it is exported as a cabinet wood known in the trade as 'porcupine wood'. The leaves can be plaited to make roofing, or stripped to the stem to make brooms or food covers.

Even the sap of the tree has its uses. Tapped fresh from the stem of a mature leaf, coconut toddy is a rich and refreshing drink. Leave it for a few days and it ferments, producing simple palm wine, which can be refined to produce a fierce spirit popular in Sri Lanka, India and Southeast Asia. Boiled and reduced, toddy becomes palm sugar, a popular constituent of many South and Southeast Asian sweets. Truly, no part of this remarkable tree is ever wasted.

Container made of coconut used for gathering toddy

Festivals and religion

Most people in Sri Lanka are Buddhists, but Hinduism has a strong preserve here as well. Islam, Christianity and other faiths also have their followers. Taking into account the diversity of cultures and ethnic groups, it is not surprising that there are numerous religious and secular festivals throughout the year. Some of these are celebrated on fixed dates, but others are calculated by the lunar calendar, which changes from year to year, having only 360 days.

This means, for example, that Muslim festivals such as Id ul-Fitr move backwards by several days each year of the international calendar, so it's impossible to state here precisely when a Muslim 'id', or festival, will occur. The only way to be sure is to ask or to buy a Muslim calendar. Muslim festivals are dependent on the sighting of the new moon. It's easier to predict Buddhist festivals, which are generally celebrated on full moon days – so, for example, the Kandy Perahera may be said to fall at full moon time in July/August. In fact, both of the major communities, Buddhist and Hindu, hold their greatest celebrations in July and August.

January
Duruthu Perahera is celebrated in Colombo. It commemorates a visit by the Buddha to Sri Lanka.

February
Navam Perahera is a colourful festival including dancers, with elephants parading the streets of Colombo in the vicinity of the Gangaramaya Temple for two days.

Independence Day is celebrated on 4 February with military parades, pageants depicting the nation's culture and achievements, dances and national games.

March
Maulud celebrates the Prophet Muhammad's birthday. Falls in February 2010.

April
Sinhala and Tamil New Year is a traditional event which marks the passage of the sun from Pisces to Aries and is celebrated island-wide with elephant races, coconut games and pillow fights between pairs of men.

May
May Day is celebrated with parades and rallies organised by the trade unions to mark International Workers' Day.

Vesak Full Moon Festival celebrates the birth, enlightenment and passing away of the Buddha with large illuminated *pandal* (floats), pageants and the distribution of food and refreshments to pilgrims.

June
Poson Full Moon Festival marks the advent of Buddhism to Sri Lanka in the 3rd century BC and is celebrated with religious observances. Illuminations, pageants and processions are part of the celebrations held in most parts of the island.

July/August
Kandy Esala Perahera is a Buddhist festival and the island's most spectacular pageant, held during a period of ten days in the hill capital of Kandy. There is a gigantic procession of hundreds of dancers, over 100 elephants clad in ceremonial attire, and hundreds of drummers and torch bearers lighting the whole city. The Esala Full Moon

Kandy Esala Perahera, Sri Lanka's biggest festival

is also celebrated in other parts of the island, with similar festivals to that in Kandy being held in Kataragama, Dondra, Bellanwila and Munneswaram. **Vel** is the main annual Hindu festival, celebrated around the island with an ornately decorated Vel chariot parading the streets, carrying the weapons of the god Skanda from one temple to another. **Kataragama** sees Hindu devotees indulge in astonishing displays of ritual self-mortification.

October
Deepavali is the festival of lights celebrated by all Hindus to honour Lakshmi.
Ramadan begins on 21 August in 2009 and 11 August in 2010.
Id ul-Fitr, celebrating the end of Ramadan, falls in September in 2009 and 2010.

November
Id ul-Adha is a Muslim festival that falls in November in 2009 and 2010.

December
Unduwap Full Moon (Sangamitta Day) commemorates the historic day on which a sapling from the tree in India under which the Lord Buddha attained enlightenment was brought to Sri Lanka. Today devotees pay homage at the Sacred Bo Tree (*see pp32–3*) in Anuradhapura, Sri Lanka's first capital. **Christmas** is also very much part of the island's festivities, and is celebrated island-wide by Christians.

Festivals and religion

Religion

Buddhism

Most Sri Lankans – 74 per cent of the population – are Buddhists. They are almost uniformly Sinhalese, and they follow the Theravada school, or 'Way of the Elders'.

Theravada Buddhism emphasises personal salvation rather than the way of the Bodhissatva associated with Mahayana teachings – that is, the temporary renunciation of personal salvation in order to help humanity achieve enlightenment. The goal of the Theravadin is to become an arhat or 'worthy one'. This is considered to be someone who has travelled the Noble Eightfold Path and, having eliminated the 'ten fetters' or erroneous mental conceptions, attains Nirvana. The Noble Eightfold Path represents the Buddhist scheme of moral and spiritual self-development leading to Enlightenment. The eight constituents are:

Right understanding
Right motivation
Right speech
Right action
Right livelihood
Right effort
Right mindfulness
Right contemplation.

At the central core of Buddhist thought lie the Four Noble Truths, which, as Gautama Buddha taught in his first lesson, had the power to liberate any human being who could attain them.

They are:

Dukkha – that there can be no existence without suffering.
Samudaya – that the cause of suffering is egoistic desire.
Nirodha – that the elimination of desire extinguishes suffering.
Magga – that the way to extinguish suffering is the Noble Eightfold Path.

Above all, honour and respect should be paid to the *triratana*, or 'Three Jewels' of Buddha, *sangha* (order of monks) and *dhamma* (sacred teachings).

Hinduism

After Buddhists, Hindus – almost all of whom are Tamils – represent the largest religious group in Sri Lanka. Hinduism

Buddhist monk praying at Gal Vihara

recognises literally dozens of deities, but the Lord Brahma is regarded as the supreme Godhead. Hinduism is a rather eclectic religion, or at least appears so to the non-Hindu. Thus the Buddha himself is readily incorporated within Hinduism as an incarnation of the great Hindu deity Vishnu. Like Buddhists, Hindus also seek to break the seemingly endless cycle of rebirth through attaining enlightenment. This can be achieved through meaningful worship, meditation, ascetic practices and selflessness.

Within Hinduism, guidance is provided by priests and gurus. In Sri Lanka the most important (and popular) Hindu deities are Skanda, the God of War; Vishnu, the Preserver of the Universe; Shiva, the Creator-Destroyer; Ganpati, the God of Wisdom; Lakshmi, the Bringer of Wealth; and Ganesh, the elephant-headed God. Hindu gods appear in many Buddhist temples, just as the Buddha may appear in Hindu temples. The religions are distinct yet linked, as they have been for perhaps as long as two millennia.

Islam

Islam is Sri Lanka's third religion. Nearly all of the country's Muslims are Moors or Malays, at around 7 per cent of the population. Sri Lankan Muslims are largely Sunni (orthodox) followers of the Shafi'i School, which predominates around the Indian Ocean littoral. There are also

Puja at Maha Devala Temple, Kataragama

small numbers of Shia Muslims, mainly Bohras and Ismailis.

Christianity

The Portuguese introduced Christianity to Sri Lanka, mainly Roman Catholicism. It is mostly visible along the west coast, especially around Negombo.

Other faiths

There are small numbers of Sikhs and Parsees in Sri Lanka. Many of the very few remaining Veddas (*see p25*) have adopted Buddhism, but their original faith was animist.

The Sacred Bo Tree

The oldest authenticated tree in the world, Sri Maha Bodhi, Anuradhapura

If there is any one tree that is universally revered in the Buddhist and Hindu world, it must be the majestic Pipal tree, a member of the family of fig trees. The tree's main claim to fame is that in about 524 BC, 29-year-old Siddhartha Gautama, a prince from Kapilavastu in today's Nepal, attained enlightenment while meditating in its shade. The memorable event happened in a small place in the present Northern Indian state of Bihar, which from that time on has been called Bodh Gaya, 'Place of Enlightenment'. Siddhartha Gautama has since become known the world over as the 'Buddha' or 'Enlightened One'.

Yet Pipal worship is not really a Buddhist invention. Pipal trees were in fact already considered sacred in pre-Buddhist days. The Hindus regarded Pipal trees as the abode of the holy trinity of Brahma, Vishnu and Shiva, who respectively are the Gods of Creation, Preservation and Destruction. In Hindu iconography, the leaves of Pipal trees have often been adorned with depictions of Lord Krishna, who is said to be an incarnation of Vishnu. Formerly, the trunks of Pipal trees were often made to 'wear' Brahmin strings – the symbolic strings habitually worn by male Brahmins, members of the highest caste in Hindu society.

Just as it has many different religious connotations, the Pipal also has many different names. In India, Nepal and Sri Lanka, it is honorifically called Bodhi or Bo Tree, the 'Tree of Enlightenment'. In non-religious language, it is simply Pipal, from Sanskrit *pippala*; to botanists it is *Ficus religiosa*, or 'Holy Fig Tree'. South Indian Christians of centuries gone by, being somewhat intimidated by the Pipal's permanently shaking leaves, named it 'Devil's Tree'. Each separate leaf was seen as being agitated by a ghost. Sri Lankan Buddhists, incidentally, being naturally more positively inclined towards the Pipal, insist that it sheds its leaves not in autumn, as might be expected, but during the full moon festival of Vesakha Poya (April/May), which commemorates Buddha's enlightenment.

The world's most famous – and probably oldest – Pipal tree can be found in Anuradhapura, Sri Lanka. In 249 BC the Buddhist monk Mahinda, son of the Indian emperor Ashoka, had come to Sri Lanka to spread Buddhism. Being a master of rhetoric, Mahinda soon converted King Devanampiya Tissa of Anuradhapura. After his conversion, the king ordered that a sapling from the Pipal tree under which Buddha had attained enlightenment to be brought to his capital. In 244 BC the nun Sanghamitta, a sister of Mahinda, arrived in a triumphant procession in Anuradhapura, carrying in her hand

A large Bo tree in a village near Anuradhapura

A monk praying at the Sacred Bo Tree in Anuradhapura

the sacred sapling the king had asked for. To celebrate its arrival, the roads in Anuradhapura were strewn with gleaming white sand.

The branch was carried to the royal garden, where a number of miracles occurred. Just as a cutting was about to be taken from the branch for the planting ceremony, it spontaneously sprang from the branch to land in a vase prepared for the occasion. After the cutting was planted in the garden, it started to rain. The deluge continued without stopping for seven days and the sapling soon became a vigorous little tree.

Today, if anything happened to the Pipal in Anuradhapura, it would be considered a national catastrophe. All Pipal trees on Sri Lankan temple grounds are supposed to have descended from this tree, which in a way is the spiritual centre of Sri Lankan Buddhism.

Impressions

Sri Lanka is simply gorgeous. Everyone agrees. On seeing the island in 1897 Mark Twain was moved to write 'Dear me, it is beautiful! And most sumptuously tropical, as to character of foliage and opulence of it'. It's also surprisingly friendly and an easy place for the English-speaker to get by. The food is good, and prices are reasonable to say the least. Were it not for the politics of communal violence that affect mainly the north and east, the island would be a little paradise in the first rank of tropical destinations.

That said, there are several Sri Lankas. On arrival, the visitor will be exposed to the bustle and busy commerce of Colombo, the island's capital and only major city. It's not to everyone's taste, and few people will choose to make it their base throughout their Sri Lankan holiday. It is worth a couple of days, though, to explore from the messy cacophony of the Pettah markets to the up-market suburbs around and beyond Cinnamon Gardens. If you're going to suffer culture shock in Sri Lanka, then it's most likely to occur soon after arriving in Colombo. From here on, it just gets better.

Sunny beaches

Stretching away south from Colombo and round beyond the southern tip of the island at Dondra Head are some of the loveliest beaches in the world. They're also geared up for tourism, with a wide range of hotels from luxurious giants to cosy, small guesthouses. Most people in this part of the country are Sinhalese, but as in the Tamil north, English is widely spoken and English-language menus offer a wide range of South Asian and international dishes. Sri Lanka has been dealing with Westerners – Portuguese, Dutch and British especially – for the best part of five centuries, and knows how to provide service and value for money.

Cool highlands

Not very far away from the tropical coasts, Sri Lanka rises suddenly into the stunningly beautiful Central Highlands. It's like a different world. The land of Robinson Crusoe is left behind, and as you climb through neat rubber and tea plantations you find yourself, unexpectedly, on Horton Plains. Here, on a cold wet day (and especially at night) you might be forgiven for thinking you were on Dartmoor, waiting for the Hound of the Baskervilles to appear! The people in these parts are more Tamil than

Impressions

Sinhalese, but if anything they're even more friendly, and once again English is very widely spoken and understood.

The dry zone

Different again is the nature of the more arid lowlands, which lie to the north of the highland belt and are home to Sri Lanka's greatest cultural treasures – magical cities from the past like Anuradhapura, Polonnaruwa and the great rock fortress of Sigiriya. Here, as on the southern beaches, the visitor needs shade, sunglasses and a good sunscreen rather than the warm clothes that may be required in the much cooler highlands.

The Tamil north

While Jaffna opened up following the 2002 ceasefire, mounting violence between 2006 and 2008 and the closure of route 9 have effectively put the north off limits. It would be unwise to travel to the lovely beaches of Nilaveli and Uppuveli near Trincomalee without first checking the security situation.

Politics

It's best to be careful when discussing politics. Most Sri Lankans are only too happy to get into a friendly political discussion, and nearly all hold definite views both about world affairs in general, and about the recent civil war in particular. Bear in mind, however, that the 2002 ceasefire was broken in 2008 and there's no great trust, let alone love, between many Tamils and Sinhalese. The Tamil LTTE (whom you're unlikely to run into in any case) are often distinguished by a fanatical loyalty to their cause (*see pp142–3*). The same is true of the Sinhalese Janatha Vimukthi Peramuna, or JVP, a group

Stilt fishermen at Ahangama on the south coast

Muslim schoolgirls at Nuwara Eliya

that somehow manages to combine elements of Buddhism, Marxism and Sinhalese nationalism. Most Sinhalese and Tamils are much more moderate, and hold views somewhere between these two extremes. Interestingly, the Tamil-speaking Moors, or Muslims, tend (on the whole) to support the Sinhalese standpoint, which in times past has earned them particularly harsh treatment from the LTTE, who regard them (being Tamil speakers) as traitors. By all means enter into political discussion with Sri Lankans you meet, but bearing the above in mind, be a little discreet, especially if some of that coconut toddy is being passed around!

Irritations and annoyances

Sri Lanka is, on the whole, an easy country to travel in, whether you're lying on the beach at Unawatuna or slogging through the mists of Horton Plains towards World's End. There are irritations and annoyances, however, and it's best to be aware of (and prepared for) these. To begin with, in Colombo – although less so elsewhere – you must be prepared for a certain amount of begging and importuning. Watch out for 'students' seeking assistance and 'gem dealers' offering surprising bargains. It's best simply not to speak to such people at all beyond a firm but polite 'no thank you'. In reality it's not all that big a problem, and much, much better than in some other parts of Asia. Watch out, too, for pickpockets and the light-fingered, especially in and around the Pettah district.

Paedophilia is an unpleasant subject, and a problem the Sri Lankan authorities are trying hard to deal with, but parts of the island (notably around Negombo and Hikkaduwa) have acquired a reputation for male prostitution, usually of quite young boys. This has drawn in numbers of undesirable predators from Europe, Australia and North America. For once, women are unlikely to be troubled by these boys or their agents, but it can be annoying and even downright infuriating for the single man. Once again, be prepared to just say 'no thank you' as politely as you can manage.

Women travellers
Unaccompanied women should dress discreetly and avoid making too much direct eye contact with Sri Lankan men, particularly those hanging about at night or in isolated places. This isn't a particular criticism of Sri Lanka, as it can be equally true of parts of London or New York. Still, discretion, as ever, is advised, and should someone trouble you, don't hesitate to let other people know that you're being bothered.

Driving
There's no doubt about it, driving in Sri Lanka is dangerous. Unfortunately it's also quite the best way to explore the island, and car hire is both relatively simple and cheap. The solution is to drive defensively, never to speed, and above all not to drive anywhere in the dark unless you really have to. Not only

A fruit stall in Tissamaharama

Curd vendor's bicycle, Pettah

are there unlit bullock carts, bicycles and pedestrians all over the place, but a very high percentage of Sri Lankan vehicles have no tail or brake lights. Watch out, in particular, for speeding buses that think they own the road. The brutal truth is that they do own it! They're bigger than you, they tend not to slow down, and it's best to just pull over onto the verge if you see one coming or one is in danger of tailgating you.

What to wear

As just about anywhere in Asia, the rule of thumb is 'dress politely'. Sri Lankan men may wear anything from an old T-shirt and sarong to very dapper, elegant suits, shirts and ties. The women, similarly, may dress traditionally in a sarong (you will soon notice that the Sinhalese women tie theirs slightly differently to the Tamils, with a frill left projecting at waist level) or they may wear designer label high fashion, particularly in Colombo. Young people of both sexes may dress casually but smartly in jeans and T-shirts or blouses. What Sri Lankans do not do is dress improperly or in a revealing fashion, and this is frowned upon by members of all the island's communities. This should apply everywhere, but especially in temples, mosques and churches, where short shorts or dresses and uncovered arms are unacceptable. Of course it's fine to wear swimsuits, including bikinis, on the beaches – although naked swimming is a no-no – but you should change into something more appropriate when entering the hotel buffet or sitting down to a meal at any restaurant that isn't right on the beach.

Rocky headland at Tangalle Bay

MIRACULOUS SURVIVAL

Kachchimalai Mosque at Beruwela, south of Colombo, was one of several religious buildings that survived the 2004 tsunami against all the odds. According to the imam, Alim Alavi, 'At the time the waves crashed, there were 47 students in the madrassa attached to the south wing of the mosque. They came running to me. I made them recite relevant stanzas from the Holy Qur'an which sought Almighty Allah's protection from natural calamities. I could see fishing trawlers drifting, buildings crumbling and even five-metre-high rocks floating. But the mosque stood unmoved despite the surging waves. It was a miracle.' The students were resident scholars of the mosque and they were subsequently sent home to overcome the trauma caused by the tragedy.

Proprieties aside, it's a good idea to wear a hat, sunglasses and strong sunscreen. Away from the beaches wear shoes rather than flip-flops/sandals, as the streets aren't always very clean (especially around markets) and even small cuts can fester quickly in a hot tropical climate.

Temples and mosques

Visitors are normally welcome in temples and mosques, although it's better to avoid entering at prayer times. Shoes should be removed and left outside in the space provided, although this does not apply to churches or the occasional Chinese temple. Some Roman Catholic churches prefer that visitors do not traipse through when services are being held.

Photography

On the whole Sri Lankans of whatever ethnic or cultural background don't mind being photographed, but when in doubt it's always better to ask. Visitors should also be careful not to photograph banks, military buildings, police stations, sentry boxes, government buildings and so on. Sri Lanka's ethnic tensions come and go, and security matters are taken very seriously indeed. Keep that camera for the beach and the Cultural Triangle!

Kachchimalai Mosque, Beruwela, survived the 2004 tsunami

Sri Lanka

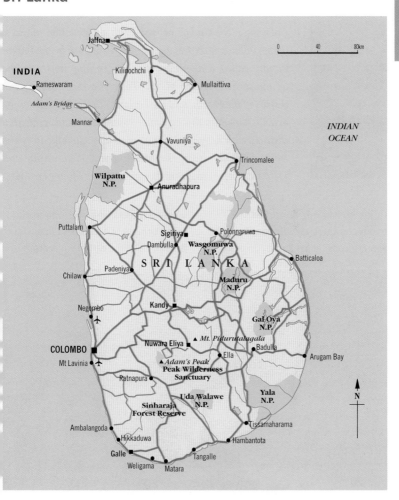

Eating and drinking

Sri Lankans generally eat with their right hand (although rich families and denizens of modern Colombo are more likely to use a knife and fork nowadays). The left hand is reserved for ablutions and should be kept well away from communal food bowls. Muslims, of course, will not eat (or serve) pork, and many Hindus as well as Buddhists are vegetarians. Alcohol is permitted, and beer or spirit drinking far from unusual (especially the ubiquitous cheap coconut toddy found throughout the country). Intoxication, though, is frowned upon, just as it is in most places.

Colombo

Colombo is Sri Lanka's capital. With a population in excess of one million, it centres on a long strip of park by the Indian Ocean called Galle Face Green. To the north is the administrative centre of the Fort, the busy commercial district of the Pettah, and the harbour. To the south Colombo extends for miles through busy commercial and residential districts with delightful Sinhalese names. Galle Road passes through Kollupitiya, Bambalapitiya, Wellawatta and Dehiwala before reaching the city limits at Mount Lavinia.

Colombo has long flourished as a major commercial centre on the western coast of Sri Lanka, drawing overseas traders from the Arab world, then Portuguese, Dutch and finally the British. Until the early 19th century

Cannon and courting couples at Galle Face Green

Colombo was overshadowed by Galle as a port, and by the inland capital of Kandy as a cultural centre. This began to change following the arrival of the British in force and the establishment of Ceylon as a Crown Colony, with Colombo as its capital, in 1802. In 1815 the last Kandyan king was deposed and exiled, while by the 1830s the British had begun the construction of a network of roads radiating across the island from Colombo. In the 1880s major construction work was begun on Colombo's harbour with the intention of developing a secure, all-weather port. When this was completed in 1907, Galle's star finally set and Colombo became the undisputed commercial and administrative heart of the nation.

Galle Face Green

Theoretically the 'green lung' of Colombo, Galle Face is a long stretch of open land, once grass, which is now so popular with local footballers, cricketers, kite-flyers and joggers that it's increasingly barren, brown earth, though attempts are being made to resuscitate it. Established in 1859 by then governor Sir Henry Ward as 'a gift for the women and children of Colombo', the promenade along the seafront is lined with old cannons, a parapet that shields courting couples and provides a perch for fishermen, and numerous hawkers and food stalls. Facing due west across the Indian Ocean, it's a fine place to visit at sunset.

GALLE FACE HOTEL

Just south of the promenade stands one of Sri Lanka's oldest and proudest institutions, the **Galle Face Hotel**. Built in 1864, this elegant and comfortable hotel has attracted many well-known guests over the years. A plaque in the foyer lists some of these celebrities, including Noël Coward, Laurence Olivier, Gregory Peck, Prince Philip and John D. Rockefeller. Recently restored and refurbished, it's a great place to stay right in the heart of Colombo. Even if you don't stay here, be sure to call in for an early-evening drink at the patio bar for an unsurpassed view of the sun setting over the Indian Ocean.

Colombo

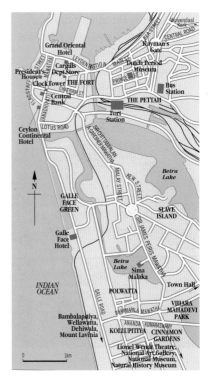

The Fort

Immediately north of Galle Face Green is the administrative and commercial heart of Colombo known as The Fort, or more often just Fort. During the Portuguese and Dutch periods this was indeed a fortified stronghold, but today no traces of fortifications remain. Instead the area is a mix of some rather fine 19th-century colonial architecture, such as the department stores **Cargills and Millers**, and modern steel-and-glass structures like the **Ceylon Continental Hotel** and the **Central Bank**. Fort is also the location of **President's House**, once the official residence but no longer in use because of the security situation. Indeed the whole Fort area is subject to very tight security, which can be a bit intimidating. The centre of the area is marked by the **Clock Tower**, originally

Plantation House, Colombo Fort

a lighthouse built in 1837, at the junction of Chatham Street and Janadhipathi Mawatha. Slightly further north, on Church Street, stands the venerable **Grand Oriental Hotel**. The view across the harbour from the fourth-floor Harbour Restaurant is memorable, but – again, for reasons of security – no photography is permitted.

The Pettah

East of Fort lies the Pettah, a name derived from the Sinhalese *pita kotuwa* or 'outside the fort'. The Pettah is really the heart of old Colombo, and a vibrant area of markets, shops, temples and mosques, which mark it both as a bustling centre of trade and an astonishing mix of peoples. Almost anything is for sale here, from fresh fruit and vegetables, through tea and herbal medicines, to clothing, watches and jewellery. Often whole streets or sections of streets are given over to specific trades such as leatherwork or brasswork. **Sea Street**, for example, is the commercial home of the Chettiar caste of goldsmiths who migrated from south India more than a century ago, while **Fifth Cross Street** seems to stock just about every spice known to humankind (*see pp48–9*). Colombo's main railway station, **Fort Station**, is in the southern part of Pettah. This is the main terminus for destinations across the country, including Kandy and the hill country.

As well as numerous temples and mosques (see the walk on *pp46–7*), the

The Clock Tower, Chatham Street, Colombo

Pettah is home to the **Wolvendaal Kerk**, built in 1749, the capital's oldest Christian place of worship. The floor is set with tombstones from an earlier Dutch church in Fort, moved here in the early 19th century. Further to the north, in the nearby Kotahena area, is **St Lucia's Cathedral**, Colombo's main Catholic church, capable of accommodating 6,000 worshippers. It seems most unlikely in this Asian capital, but the domed cathedral is dedicated to the virgin Saint Lucy of Syracuse in distant Sicily.

Walk: Temples and mosques

The Pettah is home to merchants originating from many lands and of many creeds. It's one of the best places in Sri Lanka to see Hindu temples and Muslim mosques, although there are no remarkable Buddhist temples here.

Allow 2–3 hours.

From the Khan Memorial Clock Tower on Main Street head east for about 250m (270yds) and turn left into 2nd Cross Street.

1 Masjid Jami ul-Alfar

A short distance down on the right is the elaborate, candy-striped red and white Masjid Jami ul-Alfar on 2nd Cross Street, which dates from 1909. As in mosques throughout Sri Lanka, non-Muslim visitors are most welcome, except during prayer times, but they should be modestly dressed.

Walk back down 2nd Cross Street to the south and turn left onto Main Street. Continue for around 300m (330yds) until you reach the Kayman's Gate area.

Turn left (north) onto Sea Street and pass the shops of the Chettiar goldsmiths.

2 Sea Street

Here you will find three of the Pettah's most important *kovil*, or Hindu temples, near the Goldsmiths' Bazaar. The **Old Kathiresan** and **New Kathiresan** temples are devoted to the warrior god Skanda and are worth a visit at any time but really come into their own during the Vel festival, held each July. An image of Skanda, carrying

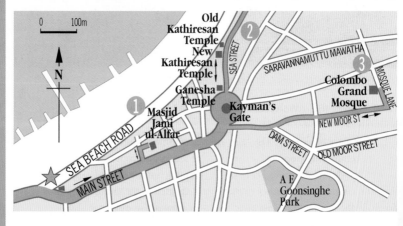

his three-pronged *vel*, or trident, is dragged on a chariot from Pettah to Bambalapitiya in the southern part of town. Nearby stands a third temple, the **Ganesha Kovil**, dedicated to the elephant-headed god Ganesh.

Make your way back to Kayman's Gate and turn east along New Moor Street. At the junction with Mosque Lane stands the capital's most important mosque.

3 Colombo Grand Mosque

The mosque dates from 1826. Enter, as ever, respectfully dressed, and ask to be shown the ceremonial cannon used to signal the breaking of fast during Ramadan, as well as the festivals of 'Id ul-Adha, marking the Hajj pilgrimage to Mecca, and 'Id ul-Fitr, marking the end of Ramadan. The area is very much a Moorish quarter.

Head south on leaving the mosque along the last 40m (45yds) of Mosque Lane and turn right along New Moor Street. Head back to Kayman's Gate and the heart of the Pettah.

Jami-ul-Alfar Mosque in Colombo

All the spices of the Indies

'And there come to these marts great ships, on account of the bulk and quantity of pepper and aromatic spices that are available there...'

Periplus Maris Erythraei, 1st century AD

Pepper is just one, if perhaps the best known, of the many spices produced in Sri Lanka to preserve or flavour much of the food we eat. Employed in small quantities to impart flavour, aroma and piquancy to food, spices are of little nutritional value, but they stimulate the appetite, enhance flavour and add zest to cooking, giving delight to gourmets and making otherwise bland foodstuffs irresistible.

While the word 'spice' is loosely used to refer to a wide variety of seasonings, true spices are the dried seeds, bark, flower parts, roots, buds or fruits of plants. Common examples, besides pepper, include

A selection of dried spices

cardamom, cinnamon, cloves, ginger, nutmeg, mace, sesame and allspice. Today, thanks to improved communications and comparative human affluence, most people can walk into the local supermarket or corner store and purchase a selection of spices for a modest outlay of cash. Such was not always the case, however. In times past spices were used not just to enhance the flavour of food, but to mask unpleasant tastes and odours. Because there were so few ways to keep food fresh, the value of spices – then a rare commodity procured with great difficulty from the uttermost ends of the earth – rose to a point that can scarcely be imagined today. To medieval Europe, a handful of Sri Lankan cinnamon was worth more than a peasant's annual wages, while slaves were bought and sold for a pinch of peppercorns!

For many centuries Arab traders enjoyed a monopoly as middlemen in the spice trade, buying pepper, cloves and other rare commodities

Spice-trading dhow off the Malabar Coast, India

from the distant markets of South Asia. These were transported across the vast expanses of the Indian Ocean to be sold in Europe at vastly inflated prices.

Not surprisingly, the Arabs were anxious to maintain their monopoly over this valuable commodity, and invented fantastic tales of the dangers and difficulties involved in obtaining spices. Not that acquiring spices was easy; the Arabs were masters of navigation, skilled traders and sophisticated businessmen whom it would be hard to circumvent. By around 1400, however, the value of spices had reached such extraordinary heights that the search for a sea route to Sri Lanka and the neighbouring Malabar Coast became a priority in Europe, with the Portuguese, Spanish, British, Dutch and French all vigorously competing to find the way. Indeed, unlikely as it may seem today, the demand for spices contributed in no small way to the 'discovery' of the New World by Columbus in 1492 and six years later, in 1498, to Vasco da Gama's arrival in the waters off Sri Lanka.

Today the massed spices available in Colombo's Pettah are available worldwide. They may not fetch the sky-high prices they once did, but they still make many a Pettah spice merchant a handsome living.

Colombo's Town Hall

Slave Island and Cinnamon Gardens

Beyond the railway lines which mark the southern limit of the Pettah is **Beira Lake**, and beyond this in turn lies a broad swathe of parks and administrative districts leading from Slave Island in the north to Vihara Mahadevi Park and then to the delightfully named **Cinnamon Gardens** in the south.

There's not a great deal to draw the visitor to **Slave Island**, which is in fact a narrow peninsula of land between two branches of Beira Lake. This area was once used to house African slaves first brought from East Africa by the Portuguese. Slavery in Sri Lanka was abolished by the British in 1845, but the name Slave Island lives on.

To the southwest of Slave Island, in the middle of the southernmost section of Beira Lake, an artificial island connected to the mainland via a causeway from Sir James Peiris Mawatha is home to **Sima Malaka**. This is a Buddhist temple based on a modernised version of traditional Kandyan style. Designed by the renowned architect Geoffrey Bawa, it features overhanging tiled roofs supported by carved wooden struts, so that the monsoon rains are excluded, but cooling breezes from the nearby Indian Ocean can blow in. It's an elegant and peaceful structure, perhaps best seen illuminated at night.

The broad east–west avenue Dharmapala Mawatha divides Slave Island from the large and attractive **Vihara Mahadevi Park**. Formerly named after Queen Victoria, this is Colombo's largest and most pleasant park and incorporates a botanical garden. There's a profusion of tropical trees and plants, as well as a fine collection of orchids. The best time to visit is between March and May, when many of the flowering trees are in bloom and the park is filled with the calls and colour of tropical birds.

Just south of the park there are a number of significant buildings and institutions, including the National Museum, the Archaeological Department and the National Art Gallery (*see opposite*). Colombo's impressive, white-domed **Town Hall** overlooks the park from the northeast. To the east, on nearby De Soysa Circus, stands the extraordinary gingerbread-style colonial Victorian Memorial Building, formerly a hospital.

Beyond the park, Maitland and Guildford Crescents mark the northern limits of Cinnamon Gardens, Colombo's most prestigious residential district and home to many of the foreign embassies based in the capital. At the southern end of Independence Avenue stands the Independence Commemoration Hall, while just a few metres to the northeast, near the junction of Independence Square and Maitland Place, is a replica of the revered and magnificent Aukana Buddha of Northern Central Province (*see p129*). It's better to see the real thing, but if you're pushed for time this replica is worthy of a visit.

Museums and art galleries

Most Colombo museums and galleries are located in the central administrative area south of Slave Island.

Dutch Period Museum

One exception is the Dutch Period Museum, located in the Pettah, which has been recently restored and provides a fascinating and informative insight into the period of Dutch rule on the island between about 1640 and 1800. *95 Prince Street, Pettah. Tel: 244 8466. Open: Tue–Sat 9am–5pm. Admission charge.*

Lionel Wendt Theatre and Art Gallery

A short walk further south of Slave Island, the Lionel Wendt Theatre and Art Gallery also puts on regular exhibitions of local Sri Lankan artists, as well as staging musical performances and plays. *18 Guildford Crescent. Tel: 269 5794. Opening times vary. Admission charge for some events.*

National Art Gallery

The National Art Gallery is located south of Vihara Mahadevi Park. It features an extensive collection of portraits, as well as exhibitions of contemporary Sri Lankan artists. *Ananda Kumaraswamy Mawatha. Tel: 269 3965. Open: Sat–Thur 9am–5pm. Closed: Fri, Sat & public holidays. Free admission.*

National Museum

The National Museum is also located south of Vihara Mahadevi Park. Opened in 1877, it houses an extensive collection of sculpture, paintings, religious and royal artefacts from all the periods of Sri Lanka's long history, from Anuradhapura, Polonnaruwa and Sigiriya, through the Kandyan Period to colonial times. If you visit any museum in Colombo, this should be the one. Don't miss the first-floor exhibition halls, which have wonderfully executed reproductions of the wall paintings at Polonnaruwa and Sigiriya. *Marcus Fernando Mawatha. Tel: 269 4767. www.museum.gov.lk. Open: Sat–Thur 9am–5pm. Admission charge.*

Natural History Museum

The Natural History Museum stands next to the National Museum and is worth a visit for those interested in Sri Lanka's natural history and geology. *Marcus Fernando Mawatha. Tel: 269 1399. Open: Sat–Thur 9am–5pm. Closed: Fri & public holidays. Admission charge.*

Tropical fruits

Much of Sri Lanka is almost unbelievably fertile, with rich shades of green the predominant colour. Whether it's rice or palm oil, hardwood or rubber, it thrives here – and that is particularly true of fruit. Visitors to the island, and especially those from cooler, temperate climates, are in for a real treat. Many of Sri Lanka's wide range of fruits can be found on supermarket shelves worldwide. Pineapples, coconuts, bananas and mangoes have long been familiar to shoppers as far afield as London and New York, but they simply don't taste as refreshing or as succulent as the same fruits fresh from the tree.

Then there are less familiar fruits which should be sampled as well. Durian, rambutan, jackfruit, mangosteen, wood apple and custard apple are just a few of the delicious varieties available locally that rarely make it to consumers in America and Europe.

There is an abundance of fruit in Sri Lanka. In the appropriate seasons, especially towards the end of the hot season in May, the markets overflow with a wide variety of exotic fruits. There's fruit to be had all year round, though, and it's generally both reasonably priced and safe (if carefully washed with bottled water). Fresh fruit is available for sale almost everywhere, but two of the larger fruit markets in Colombo are Pettah Market and Kollupitiya Market.

Visitors to Sri Lanka who see unfamiliar fruits for sale in shops and markets shouldn't be shy – ask the name, and whether you can sample a piece. Sri Lankans are friendly and generous; they're also

Jackfruit, Balangoda

A fruit and vegetable stall in Talawakele

proud of the bounty that nature has given their island, and respond warmly to such enquiries.

Watch out for the notorious durian, though – with this fruit it's a case of love it or hate it! Many find the powerful aroma of the ripe fruit unbearable, and in some places air-conditioned buildings and public transport are 'durian-free zones'. Others find it irresistibly delicious, and are prepared to pay serious sums of money for the most prized species. It is certainly difficult to remain neutral about the durian. About the size of a football, and spiked like a medieval mace, it is held in high esteem by most Sri Lankans and is often described as 'the king of fruits'. The soft, yellow flesh concealed within is prized for its unusual and strangely addictive taste, which is said to combine the flavours of caramel, onion, cream cheese and sherry. According to some aficionados, 'It is a terrible thing if a person lives his life without knowing love, and an equally terrible thing to live a life without tasting durian'. It is also believed that the durian is a powerful aphrodisiac, hence an old adage: 'When the durians are down, the sarongs are up.'

Kollupitiya and Bambalapitiya

Beyond Galle Face Hotel, Colombo stretches away south for miles beside the Indian Ocean. A convenient railway line runs from Fort Station in the Pettah south past Slave Island to meet the coast just south of the Galle Face Hotel. From here it continues all the way to Matara in the south of the island, stopping at each of Colombo's southern coastal suburbs en route.

The first of these districts is Kollupitiya, home to a large and bustling market near the junction of Galle Road and Ananda Kumaraswamy Mawatha. Just east of **Kollupitiya Market**, along Ananda Kumaraswamy towards Vihara Mahadevi Park, is the **Sri Lanka Buddhist Information Centre**, an excellent place to visit if you're interested in learning about Sri Lanka's major religious tradition.

The next stop on the coastal railway is Bambalapitiya, a bustling and prosperous commercial district far enough away from central Colombo to feel rather off the tourist track, but with many reasonably priced guesthouses and small hotels. There are no real sights here beyond the **Vajiraramaya Mawata**, a large and important Buddhist temple located on Primrose Gardens just east of Galle Road near Havelock Town.

Wellawatta and Dehiwala

And so the railway continues, running right by the shore through Wellawatta,

A vegetable stallholder at the Kollupitiya market in Colombo

One of the lions in Dehiwala Zoo, Colombo

the first residential district in southern Colombo with pretensions to a beach, although, truth be told, there's no good bathing available until Mount Lavinia, several kilometres further to the south.

Next comes Dehiwala, home to **Dehiwala Zoo**, one of the most attractive zoological gardens in South Asia, though it will still sadden most people to see big cats and primates in cages, however well fed and treated. The zoo has a large collection of animals, both Sri Lankan and from overseas, as well as an aquarium, an aviary, a nocturnal house and a butterfly park. The main attraction is the elephant show, staged every day at 4.30pm, although again the sight of these intelligent creatures performing circus-like tricks has become increasingly incongruous in the 21st century.

The Dehiwala elephants are currently being taught to paint using their trunks. The resultant artworks will cost several hundred pounds each, but the money raised goes towards food and medical care for the elephants, both here and at the Pinnawela Orphanage (*see pp74–5*). *Dehiwala Zoo, Karagampitiya, Galle Road. Tel: 271 2751.*
Open: daily 8am–6pm.
Admission charge.

Mount Lavinia Hotel, south of Colombo

Mount Lavinia

Beyond Dehiwala, at the southern limits of metropolitan Colombo, is Mount Lavinia. Here, about 12km (7¹/₂ miles) from Colombo Fort, there is a distinct headland dominated by the

SRI JAYAWARDENAPURA-KOTTE

The legislative and judicial capital of Sri Lanka is not Colombo, but Sri Jayawardenapura-Kotte. Named after the former Kingdom of Kotte (1371–1597), the site of the former city (which was the first to establish friendly relations with the Portuguese) is today little more than a suburb of Colombo, located 11km (7 miles) southeast of the city centre. There are scarcely any traces of the old capital to be found.

Today Sri Jayawardenapura-Kotte ('City of Victory-Fort') is a modern, planned town with a large administrative complex, residential zones and public housing.

prestigious **Mount Lavinia Hotel**, long considered one of the nation's top resorts. This far south of the city centre the beach is quite pleasant and the water clean enough to permit swimming, but as with much of the west coast there's a strong undertow, and the waves can often be really rough. It may be wiser to consider the Mount Lavinia Hotel swimming pool as an alternative to the sea – non-residents can use it for a small fee.

As befits so venerable an institution, the Mount Lavinia has a distinguished past. It is thought that the original core of the building was a bungalow established in 1806 by the then British Governor of Ceylon, Sir Thomas Maitland, for his wife – or, by some accounts, lover – Lavinia. In the 1820s he had the bungalow significantly enlarged to create what is still known as 'the Governor's Wing'. Still later he was obliged to sell the place as the authorities in London disapproved of his considerable expenditure on the property and would not agree to fund so extravagant a lifestyle. Today the hotel has been lovingly maintained and seems the very essence of the colonial tropics, with elaborately decked-out servants, a private beach and a fine terrace bar with views across the Indian Ocean. It may be expensive by Sri Lankan standards, but to a visitor from Europe or North America it seems very reasonable given the facilities on offer and its unmatched location so near to Colombo.

Beyond Mount Lavinia both Galle Road and the railway line head south to **Moratuwa**, the gateway to the West Coast resorts south of Colombo (*see pp70–79*).

The northern suburbs

There is little to interest the visitor in the extensive suburbs of Colombo stretching north from the harbour towards Bandaranaike International Airport and the popular beach resort and fishing town of **Negombo** (*see p71*). Abdul Cader Road leads north along the coast from the Pettah before turning into St Anthony's Mawatha. Between the Pettah and the wide mouth of the Kelani Ganga, which enters the sea about 5km (3 miles) north of the Fort, lies a clutter of shipyards, factories and small commercial buildings. Traffic can be bad all the way out to the airport at Katunayake, about 30km ($18^1/2$ miles) distant, and apart from a few temples – notably **Muthumariamman Kovil** on Kotahena Street, which is dedicated to Pattini, Hindu goddess of health and chastity – there is relatively little to see.

The suite in the Governor's Wing, Mount Lavinia Hotel

Tour: Kelaniya

If you're interested in seeing some really fine Buddhist art and architecture near Colombo visit the Raja Maha Vihara at Kelaniya, about half an hour's drive to Colombo's northeast. Head along the Kandy Road before taking an east turn at Peligayoda to Kelaniya, about 12km (7¹/₂ miles) from Colombo Fort. It's possible to go by bus, but much easier to hire a taxi or ask your hotel reception desk to make arrangements.

Allow 2–3 hours for your visit.

At Kelaniya you will find the **Raja Maha Vihara**, probably the most venerated (and visited) temple in Sri Lanka after Kandy's Temple of the Tooth (*see pp61–2*). The temple has been instrumental in spreading Theravada Buddhism not only throughout Sri Lanka, but in mainland Southeast Asia as well. The exact date of Kelaniya's origins are not known, but according to the *Mahavansa*, an ancient Pali text, the Buddha himself visited the site on two occasions. Although Kelaniya has been a place of

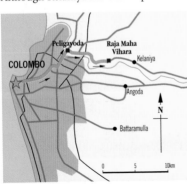

Buddhist worship for over 2,000 years, the temple buildings were mainly constructed between 1880 and 1940.

Raja Maha Vihara dominates a small mound on a plain by the banks of the Kelani River. At the foot of the steep flight of steps facing the river are guardstones, each with a bas-relief Naga king holding a flowerpot and a twisted vine. On either side of the king, in the lower corners, are two dwarfs. These are called *yakkha* and are believed to be spirit attendants of Kuvera, god of wealth.

At the top of the steps, beneath a stately triple archway are the three great symbols of the 'Triple Gem' of Buddhism. To the right is the *dagoba*, representing the physical existence of the Buddha. In the centre is the main temple, representing the community of monks, or *sangha*. On the left is a Pipal tree, symbolising the Buddha's enlightenment and attainment of nirvana (*see pp32–3*).

Crowds of devotees move through the temple, dropping a handful of rice into an urn as a symbolic offering, lighting incense, and bringing their children for blessings from the monks. In contrast to the rich colours in the rest of the temple, a painting of a blue sky with a single mountain peak backs the innermost shrine, called the 'Hall of Perfumes'. A semi-transparent piece of white gauze hangs between the small, golden, seated Buddha image and the worshippers, who prostrate themselves and sit in silent prayer or contemplation.

Raja Maha Vihara temple, Kelaniya

Kandy

With a population of around 170,000, Kandy is Sri Lanka's second-biggest city and the cultural centre of the whole island. For about two centuries (until 1815) it was the capital of Sri Lanka. Visit the famous 'Temple of the Tooth', or Sri Dalada Maligawa, where what is believed to be one of the Buddha's teeth is preserved and ardently revered. Then take a walk around adjacent Kandy Lake and its green surroundings, relaxing in the tranquil atmosphere.

Just off Kotugodalle Veediya is the unusual and attractive **Kataragama Devale**, a Hindu temple. Further afield to the west are three attractive temples of cultural significance, the **Galadeniye Vihara**, **Lankatilake Vihara** and **Embekke Devale** (*see pp66–7*). Kandy is the most important teaching centre and

Kandy

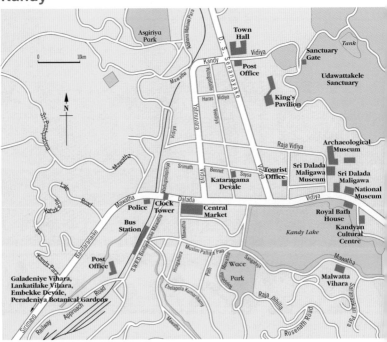

cultural repository in the country for a whole range of Sri Lankan traditions, including dance, music, handicrafts and religious practices. It's the venue for the country's most important and impressive festival, the annual Kandy Esala Perahera. Nearby are the wonderful **Peradeniya Botanical Gardens**, founded in 1371 and among the finest in the world (*see p67*).

Sri Dalada Maligawa

The most important religious and historical monument in Kandy, if not in all Sri Lanka, is the Sri Dalada Maligawa, or Temple of the Tooth. Located on the north side of Kandy Lake, the temple in its present form dates from the period of the Kandyan Kingdom, being constructed in stages between 1687 and 1782. It was severely damaged by a terrorist bomb in 1998, but has since been reconstructed. An impressive gilded roof to cover the relic chamber was presented by former President Premadasa, who was assassinated in 1993.

The Sacred Tooth is said to have been recovered from the ashes following the Buddha's cremation in 543 BC and to have been taken to Sri Lanka in the 4th century AD. Initially it was kept at Anuradhapura, but ended up in Kandy, where it remained until the Portuguese arrived in the 16th century. In a burst of religious iconoclasm the tooth was supposedly seized and taken to Goa where it was reportedly burned by the Catholic authorities. The Kandyans deny this, however, claiming that the Portuguese were tricked into taking away a false tooth, while the real relic was hidden and subsequently enshrined with great pomp and ceremony in the relic chamber of the Sri Dalada Maligawa.

The Temple of the Tooth is the most important of Kandy's monuments

Today the temple is the spiritual and cultural heart of Kandy, visited by a constant stream of pilgrims (and tourists) from early morning to sunset. Formal prayer offerings, or *puja*, are held at 6am, 10am and 6pm, and these are the best times to visit. Remember to dress respectfully with upper arms and legs covered – this is not a place for T-shirts and shorts. As in all Buddhist temples, shoes should be removed before entering. Be prepared, too, for bag and body searches, an unfortunate consequence of the civil war and of the 1998 bombing. The *puja* are accompanied by a wild cacophony of drum beats and wind instruments, highly evocative of the holy mystery surrounding the tooth and producing an atmosphere which, to the visitor, is both astonishing and exotic.

Sri Dalada Maligawa, Dalada Vidiya. Open: daily dawn–dusk. Admission charge.

Museums

Behind the main temple is the **Sri Dalada Maligawa Museum**. Here the visitor can see an extensive collection of often elaborate and bejewelled gifts to the temple, as well as historical pictures (including photos of the bomb damage caused in 1998) and a huge stuffed elephant, the 'Maligawa Tusker', dressed in full array for the Kandy Esala Perahera (*see p29*).
Open: Tue–Sat 9am–5pm. Closed: Sun, Mon & public holidays. Admission charge.

Nearby are the **National Museum** and the **Archaeological Museum**, housing regalia from the former Kandyan royal family and a copy of the 1815 treaty transferring sovereignty over Kandy to the British authorities. *Dharmapala Mawatha. Open: Tue–Sat 9am–5pm. Closed: Sun, Mon & public holidays. Admission charge.*

THE TOOTH OF THE BUDDHA IN 1819

The visitor to the Sri Dalada Maligawa today can stand within feet of the precious relic chamber and watch the ceremonies honouring the tooth, but they are not likely to get to see the relic itself. Fortunately, in 1819 the British physiologist and anatomist John Davy was present in Kandy when the sacred tooth, which had been seized by rebels, was restored to its rightful place in the Sri Dalada Maligawa. Davy subsequently recorded:

'Through the kindness of the governor, I had an opportunity (enjoyed by few Europeans) of seeing this celebrated relic… Never was a relic more preciously enshrined; wrapped in pure sheet-gold, it was placed in a case just large enough to receive it, of gold, covered externally with emeralds, diamonds and rubies, tastefully arranged. This beautiful and very valuable bijou was put into a very small gold *karandua*, richly ornamented with rubies, diamonds, and emeralds; this was enclosed in a larger one also of gold, and very prettily decorated also with rubies. This second, surrounded with tinsel, was placed in a third, which was wrapped in muslin; and this in a fourth, which was similarly wrapped; both these were of gold, beautifully wrought, and richly studded with jewels. Lastly the fourth *karandua*, about a foot and a half high, was deposited in the great *karandua*.'
John Davy, An Account of the Interior of Ceylon (1821)

Robert Knox

The almost legendary kingdom of Kandy remained pretty much a mystery until the British conquest of the region in 1815. Yet as early as 1660 an English sailor, Robert Knox, was captured by the King of Kandy and taken to the highland capital as a prisoner, where he remained for almost 20 years. On his escape and return to England he published his monumental *Historical Relation of Ceylon* (1681), which remains the most important source we have regarding the history of the independent Kingdom of Kandy (1597–1815).

Knox first landed in Sri Lanka at the mouth of the Mahaweli Ganga, near Trincomalee, where he was promptly taken prisoner by soldiers of King Rajasinha II. He was taken to Kandy, where he was surprised to find numerous other European prisoners, Dutch, French and Portuguese as well as English, who were allowed a large degree of personal freedom provided they remained within the Kingdom of Kandy and conformed to court etiquette.

In fact Knox didn't fare too badly during his long stay in Kandy. He was permitted to start a business and to buy a house. He was told that he was free to marry but chose not to as he didn't want to form personal ties which might preclude the possibility of escape. He noted, however, that extramarital relationships were easy to form and socially tolerated. In part this was because of local caste-based custom, which permitted men of higher caste to form liaisons with women of lower caste, but not to marry them.

Knox writes that the people lived a simple life, with rice as their staple diet accompanied by a variety of curried dishes, chiefly vegetable, but sometimes fish or meat.

Rajasinha appears to have been a fairly just king, though executions – including crushing by elephant – were not unknown. Even so, Knox longed for his freedom, and in 1679 he escaped to the Dutch-controlled north of the island and made his way back to England. His account of the Kingdom of Kandy is in places imbued with the European prejudices of the time, but on balance he liked the ordinary people he lived amongst, considering them 'proper and well-favoured… active and nimble in their limbs, very ingenious, very hardy [and] not very malicious towards one another'.

Around Kandy

There's nothing to match the Temple of the Tooth elsewhere in Kandy, but the town is both pleasingly attractive and intriguing. The road around the lake, which makes a pleasant and tranquil walk, has no major buildings beyond the **Malwatta Vihara**, a Buddhist monastery due south of the Sri Dalada Maligawa. Nearby is the **Hotel Suisse**, a former British governor's house dating from the mid-19th century, now converted into an attractive, colonial-style hotel. The bustling heart of Kandy is to the northwest of the lake. Here are the markets, mosques, churches and most of the restaurants. After the Temple of the Tooth, perhaps the most interesting attraction in town is the Kataragama Devale, located just off Kotugodalle Vidiya. Dedicated to Skanda, the Hindu God of War, this temple has some truly exquisite carvings, paintings and tilework.

To the south of the Temple of the Tooth, the **Kandyan Cultural Centre** does an excellent job of preserving and promoting the cultural traditions of Sri Lanka, and more especially of Kandy. Opened in 1984, it maintains a cultural museum and puts on regular displays of Kandyan classical dance and music, as well as fire-walking. *Victoria Rd. Open: daily 9am–5pm. Admission charge.*

Kandy Lake with the Temple of the Tooth (Sri Dalada Maligawa) among the trees

Monk at Malwatta Vihara, Kandy

The western temples

The most important and interesting sights in the vicinity of Kandy are in the hills to the southwest of the city, along Route 1, where three Buddhist temples (with some close Hindu associations) make a fine day's outing.

The first temple is **Embekke Devale**, about 10km (6 miles) from Kandy. Dating from the 14th century, it boasts fine wooden pillars with carvings of animals, birds, dancers and wrestlers which are thought originally to have been pillars in a royal audience hall of the Kandyan kings.
Open: daily 8.30am–5pm.
Admission charge.

From here it's a pleasant 2km (1¼-mile) walk to the **Lankatilake Vihara**, a Buddhist-Hindu temple with murals dating from the period of the Kingdom of Kandy (1600–1800), stone inscriptions and a Kandyan-style

Kandy environs

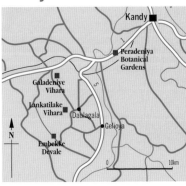

Buddha image. The views across the hills are spectacular.
Open: daily 8.30am–5pm.
Admission charge.

Temple number three is the **Galadeniye Vihara**, just 2km (1¼ miles) from Lankatilake and again within easy walking distance. This is a Buddhist temple with a separate annexe for Hindus built on a rocky outcrop

A carving at Embekke Devale Temple entrance

Galadeniye Vihara Temple

and dating from the 13–14th centuries. The main feature outside the temple is an intricate moonstone marking the entranceway.
Open: daily 8.30am–5pm. Admission charge.

Peradeniya Botanical Gardens

Just 7km (4¼ miles) out of Kandy on Route 1 to Colombo, Peradeniya Botanical Gardens have a good claim to be the oldest and best gardens in Asia. Covering an area of around 60 hectares (148 acres) and hemmed in on three sides by the waters of the Mahaweli Ganga, they are beautiful and very well maintained. Initially founded by the kings of Kandy as royal pleasure gardens, they were developed as a true botanic garden during the 19th century by the British authorities and now boast around 4,000 species.

There's a great deal to be seen here, from giant fig trees and royal palms to the 'double coconut' of the rare coco de mer (indigenous to the Seychelles) and elaborate spice gardens. It's another great day trip from Kandy, and there's a good restaurant at the **Royal Botanical Gardens Cafeteria** near the entrance. You won't find it cheap by Sri Lankan standards but there is tasty food on the fairly extensive menu. Pick up a copy of the reasonably priced and highly informative *Illustrated Guide to the Royal Botanic Gardens* at the entrance, as this identifies the major attractions and suggests popular walks through the park. *Sirima Bandaranaike Mawatha. Open: daily 9am–5.30pm. Admission charge.*

The bounteous banana

'The Plantain I take to be the King of all Fruit'
William Dampier, *Voyages* (1686)

Bananas have been around a long time, at least in the Old World of Asia, Africa and Europe. Quite where they originated remains uncertain. Some authorities favour West Africa, since the name 'banana' is believed to have come from Guinea, via Spanish and Portuguese. In all probability, though, bananas – and their equally useful green cousins, plantains – originated in Asia, possibly in Sri Lanka. Certainly bananas are noted with approval in early Greek, Latin and Arab literature, and the name plantain is believed to derive from the Latin *planta*, 'a spreading sucker or shoot'. Alexander the Great saw – and no doubt tasted – bananas on his expedition to India in the 3rd century BC, and they are mentioned in Chinese lists of Tang-dynasty exotica as pleasant fruits of *nan-yang*, or the Southern Ocean, more than 1,300 years ago.

By any yardstick the banana must rank as one of the most useful plants known to mankind. It looks like a fruit-bearing tree, but is in fact a giant herb that springs from an underground stem, known as a rhizome, to form a 'false trunk' anything from 3–9m (10–30ft) high. In other words, it's more like a stick of celery or a giant leek than a woody tree.

Bananas thrive naturally on deep, loose, well-drained soils in humid tropical climates, and they are easily cultivated with simple irrigation techniques in semi-arid regions, notably in the north and centre of Sri Lanka. Within nine to fifteen months of planting, a large flower spike,

Balangoda bananas

Even the flower of the banana is edible

bearing numerous reddish petals, emerges at the top of the false trunk and hangs downwards to become bunches of 50 to 150 individual fruits, known as fingers. These individual fruits are generally grouped in clusters known, appropriately enough, as hands. The ripe fruits contain as much as 22 per cent carbohydrate, mainly as sugar, and is high in potassium, low in protein and fat, and a good source of vitamins C and A.

Although most commonly eaten fresh, bananas may be fried, or mashed and chilled for pies and puddings. They may also be used to flavour muffins, cakes or breads in Sri Lanka (and across Southeast Asia). The flower, too, may be eaten when boiled, as indeed can the central stem of the false trunk, which provides a nutritious, if bland, base for some South Asian curries.

The leaves have many practical uses, too. They provide temporary waterproof roofing, and are used as wrapping in steaming or barbecuing food in Sri Lankan cooking. More recently, environmentally friendly wrapper bags made from specially cured banana leaves are being used to replace the ubiquitous plastic bag. The bags can be stored in a refrigerator for about a week.

Early Oriental Christians believed that leaves from the banana tree were used by Adam and Eve to fashion aprons for themselves when they were cast out from the Garden of Eden (and onto Adam's Peak in Sri Lanka – *see pp114–15*), hence the botanical name, *Musa paradisaica*, 'the banana of paradise'. The botanical gardens at Peradeniya grow a remarkably wide range of banana plants.

The west coast

North of Colombo the fishing port of Negombo, located around 40km (25 miles) from the capital and just 8km (5 miles) from Bandaranaike International Airport at Katunayaka, was Sri Lanka's first beach resort. Today it remains a major destination, but more because of its proximity to the capital and the airport than because it can properly compete with more distant and certainly more pristine resorts like Unawatuna, Tangalle and Arugam Bay. It's a fairly large town, with an impressive fishing fleet and some interesting handicraft industries.

About 50km (31 miles) further north the town of **Chilaw** is strongly and visibly Roman Catholic, but has little to offer the visitor. Not so many tourists travel north of Chilaw nowadays, although this may change if the peace process progresses well. Highway 3 leads past Mundal Lake along the coast to the fishing port and market town of **Puttalam** on the shores of Puttalam Lagoon. On a narrow spit of land to the west, protecting the lagoon from the Indian Ocean, are the small but historic settlements of **Talawila** and **Kalpitiya**. North of Puttalam Route 3 ceases and a dirt track leads to **Wilpattu National Park**. The latter is still pretty much off limits because of LTTE activities in the area, so always check before visiting. Once in Puttalam there's not much to do except return to Colombo, or take Route 12 to the Cultural Triangle centre of Anuradhapura (*see pp127–9*).

South of Colombo, beyond **Dehiwala–Mount Lavinia** (*see p56*), coastal Route 2 (in effect Galle Road) passes through the important Buddhist centre of **Kalutara** and the early Muslim settlement of **Beruwela** on its way to the historic settlement of Galle (*see pp80–85*). Interesting though these may be, however, the overwhelming attraction of this southwest coast is the beach resorts. The most important of these are **Bentota**, **Kosgoda**, **Ambalangoda** (with its fine mask museum), **Telwatta**, **Hikkaduwa** and **Dodanduwa**. These are places to kick back and relax – sea, sun and seafood are the name of the game, not cultural activities.

Inland from Negombo the **Pinnawela Elephant Orphanage** near Kegalla has an irresistible appeal, while those in search of ancient history can visit the Vijayasundarama Tooth Relic at **Dambadeniya**. For gardening enthusiasts or botanists there are the **Henaratgoda**

The west coast

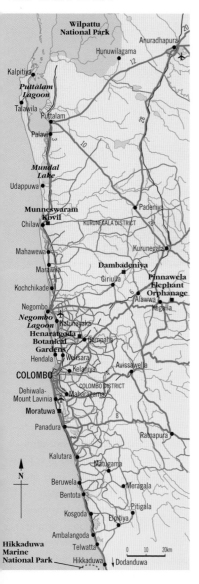

Negombo

A sizeable town with a population in excess of 125,000, Negombo strives to combine tourist appeal with a major fishing fleet, and the result doesn't always work. Certainly Negombo is a good place for nightlife at all-in resorts and for its choice of restaurants, and there are plenty of sandy beaches available for sunbathing. The water, however, is not nearly as clean as in smaller, more remote resorts, and Negombo should not be considered a diving or snorkelling destination.

The town itself fairly bustles with business. The heart of town lies along a narrow strip of land between Negombo Lagoon and the sea, and is further defined by the north–south Hamilton Canal. The front, which is called **King George's Drive**, is very much part of the fishing port at its southern end. Here you will find the large **Fish Market** and also the remains of a once powerful Dutch fort, which has a gateway still inscribed with the date 1678. Between the fort and the fish market is **The Esplanade**, an open, green area much used for that Sri Lankan sporting obsession, cricket.

As the presence of a Dutch fort indicates, Negombo is an historic town, first occupied by the Portuguese, and later captured by the Dutch in 1644 and the British in turn in 1796. The Portuguese influence is most clearly felt in the strong Roman Catholic presence. There are numerous churches in and around town, but the main one is **St Mary's** near the junction of Main Street

Botanical Gardens near Gampaha, and further south the Palace and Berendi Kovil at **Avissawella** hold appeal.

Outrigger fishing boats on the beach at Negombo

and the Hamilton Canal. A few small Catholic shrines are also dotted about town. By contrast, a Dutch influence is most apparent in the civil structure of the town, from the old **Dutch Fort** to the extensive network of old Dutch canals connecting the lagoon to other inland waterways. These canals are really quite impressive, extending all the way from Colombo in the south to Puttalam in the north – a total distance of more than 120km (75 miles). There are also a few surviving Dutch period houses near the waterfront, including the **Lagoon Resthouse** on Custom House Road.

The main hotel and entertainment strip is along the beach running north of town. Here, in Lewis Place and along Porutota Road, are most of the better places for accommodation, eating out and entertainment. If you're staying here be sure to rise early at least one morning to view Negombo's substantial fishing fleet sailing out of the lagoon and up the coast. Massed outrigger canoes known as *oruva* sweep out to sea in search of all manner of fish, including shark, tuna and swordfish, returning in the late afternoon against the setting sun. It's quite a sight and, combined with the crab, lobster and crayfish caught on a daily basis offshore and in the lagoons, should ensure some memorable seafood dishes during your stay. You can also arrange trips on *oruva* with local fishermen at very reasonable rates; check near the Fish Market or ask at your hotel reception desk.

Around Negombo

Southeast of town along the Colombo Road is the **Angurukaramulla Temple** with a 6m (20ft) long reclining Buddha. If you're exploring around Negombo, it makes sense to stay off the busy Colombo Road, however. Just south of town is the large Negombo Lagoon, and if you head south along the little-used coast road to **Pamunugawa** and **Hendala** you will avoid the heavy traffic centred on Bandaranaike International Airport at Katunayaka. It's a beautiful drive along the coast, studded with coconut palms and small churches – the entire area remains strongly Catholic. At the southern end of Negombo Lagoon is a protected wetland area called **Muthurajawela Marshlands**. This saline area is a birdwatchers' paradise, with herons, cormorants and kingfishers aplenty.

North to Wilpattu

North of Negombo, Highway 3 runs parallel to the coast to Chilaw and Puttalam. It's a lovely drive, and little frequented nowadays, since Wilpattu National Park, just north of Puttalam, remains an occasional centre of LTTE activity, so most tourists head south. Hopefully things will soon change, but for the moment it's certainly quite safe to head north as far as Puttalam, but it would be unwise to go more than 30km (19 miles) into Wilpattu National Park without a guide.

Chilaw and Puttalam

Beyond Mahawewa it's just a 20-minute drive along Chilaw Lagoon to the small, visibly Roman Catholic town of Chilaw. There's little reason to stay in this somewhat scruffy fishing port, but it can make an interesting stopover for its bustling fruit and vegetable market, as well as the **Munneswaram Kovil** about 5km (3 miles) east of town. There's a major festival here in August when devotees of the Hindu god Shiva walk along banks of red-hot coals, apparently unscathed. About 12km ($7^1/2$ miles) north of Chilaw on Route 3

BATIK PRODUCTION

The small town of Marawila straddles Highway 3 about 25km ($15^1/2$ miles) north of Negombo and around 3km (2 miles) inland from the Indian Ocean. Together with the nearby town of Mahawewa, about 5km (3 miles) further north, this area of palm trees and rice paddies is known for its batik production. You don't need to come here to buy batik – it's for sale all over the island, especially in Colombo, Negombo and the southern resorts – but it's a good place to visit to see the process of manufacture. There are a number of up-market hotels dotted along the coast in this area, but it also makes a perfect day trip from Negombo.

Batik making near Mahawewa

to Puttalam is another important Hindu complex, the **Udappuwa Kovil**. Once again, a fire-walking ceremony is held here each August – enquire at your hotel reception in Negombo.

For the present, the last real stop on the west coast going north is the old pearling and fishing town of **Puttalam**. It's an ancient settlement, known for its Portuguese (and indeed Mozambican) settlers from the 16th century, but today there's little to hold the traveller apart from some adequate (but not very special) accommodation and restaurants if you're driving northeast to **Anuradhapura**.

About 5km (3 miles) south of Puttalam a narrow road leads west from the small village of **Palavi** to the narrow spit of land which forms the west side of Puttalam's extensive lagoon. Here, amidst saltpans and palm groves, the small, predominantly Catholic town of **Talawila** has a church and shrine honouring St Anne; a statue of the saint in the church is believed to work miracles. Major festivals are held here in both March and July when flocks of Catholic pilgrims descend on the town, though St Anne also has Buddhist, Hindu and Muslim devotees. Further north, on the edge of Dutch Bay, is the predominantly Muslim fishing town of **Kalpitiya**. Here a Dutch fort (dating from 1667), built to guard the entrance to Puttalam Lagoon, is now a naval base.

If you do decide to head north from Puttalam into the wilds of Wilpattu National Park, the main gate is at Hunuwilagama on Route 12 between Puttalam and Anuradhapura. The park, which is Sri Lanka's largest, is home to a cross section of wildlife including leopards, crocodiles, dugongs, wild boar and deer, as well as much bird life. Unfortunately the park had to be closed in the mid-1980s because of LTTE activity in the area, and it did not reopen until 2003. At present it's considered safe to drive (with a guide) around 30km (19 miles) into the park, although you may prefer to opt for safer Yala National Park in the southeast (*see pp138–9*). It's best to make arrangements for transport and guide at your Anuradhapura hotel rather than in Puttalam.

Pinnawela Elephant Orphanage

Inland from Negombo, about 65km (40 miles) on the route to Kegalla, is the Pinnawela Elephant Orphanage. This can also easily be reached along Route 1 from Colombo and Kandy, or via Route 6 from Kurunegala. Allow 5–6 hours to drive.

If you're at all interested in elephants – which are held in great esteem throughout Sri Lanka – then Pinnawela is just about irresistible. A government-run institution, the elephant orphanage was set up to look after the abandoned or orphaned offspring of wild elephants. With somewhere around 70 baby and young elephants in the camp at any one time, it has naturally developed into the major

The Elephant Orphanage at Pinnawela

elephant attraction on the island, and makes a great day tour from Negombo, Colombo or Kandy.

The young elephants are cared for by elephant-minders or *mahouts*, and are allowed to roam throughout the camp area pretty much at will. Visitors should aim to reach Pinnawela either early in the morning, or around noon, to fit in with elephant bathing and feeding times. Bathing times are from 10am to noon and from 2pm to 4pm. Meal times are scheduled for 9.15am, 1.15pm and 5pm, so it's not such a hard life for the rescued babies, most of whom will become working elephants in adulthood.

The whole enterprise has been carefully aimed at visitors, so there are tourist shops, a restaurant, and a branch of Hatton National Bank where you can change money. There are also a couple of spice gardens in the vicinity where you can learn about tropical spices and their cultivation (*see pp48–9*) and even buy a sample or two.

Pinnawela Elephant Orphanage, Rambukkana Road. Tel: (035) 226 6116, (011) 271 7913. www.luckysama.de. Open: daily 8.30am–6pm. Admission charge.

Dambadeniya

Not far from the Negombo–Kurunegala Road, and best reached via the small road leading north from Alawwa on Route 6, is the **Tooth Relic Temple** at Dambadeniya. This can also be reached directly by back roads from Negombo via Makandura and Giriulla, but only by car or motorbike. For a short period of time during the 13th century Dambadeniya was the capital of King Parakramabahu II (1236–70). Here you will find the **Vijayasundarama Temple**,

The great *dagoba* of the Gangatilaka Vihara, Kalutara

once used to exhibit the sacred Buddha tooth relic, which still houses murals said to date from its brief period of glory in the 13th century.

Henaratgoda Botanical Gardens

About 18km (11 miles) south of Negombo on the Colombo Road, just north of the busy market town of Ja-Ela, a road leads eastwards to Henaratgoda Botanical Gardens, located close by the town of Gampaha. Although long superseded as a botanical attraction by Peradeniya Botanical Gardens near Kandy (*see p67*), Henaratgoda is conveniently located close to Colombo and Negombo and is well worth a visit. This was the place where rubber trees, originally brought from South America, were first cultivated in South Asia.

Avissawella Palace and Berendi Kovil

Almost directly due east of Colombo, about 60km (37 miles) along Route 4 to Ratnapura, the Palace and Berendi Kovil at Avissawella lie on the border between the west coast and the Central Highlands. This was the former seat of King Rajasinghe I, who resisted the Portuguese invaders and died in 1593. His former palace is now little more than an earthen mound, but the Berendi Kovil he commissioned, although unfinished, survives and exhibits some fine stone carving.

South to Kalutara

Route 2 (Galle Road) along the coast south of Colombo runs through resort after resort, all the way to the historic town of Galle (*see pp80–85*). As a general rule, the further south the less crowded the resort, but this is changing fast and once-small fishing villages like Hikkaduwa are now bustling destinations. Kalutara, just 40km (25 miles) south of Colombo, is more notable for its location at the mouth of the broad Kalu Ganga and the presence of a major Buddhist temple, the **Gangatilaka Vihara**, than as a beach resort. Still, it's a good place to stop on the way south and perhaps have lunch by the Kalu Ganga after visiting the impressive and obviously wealthy temple.

Beruwela and Bentota

Situated 60km (37 miles) and 66km (41 miles) south of Colombo

ENDANGERED TURTLES

Six separate breeds of turtle lay their eggs along this coast, and all are endangered – hence the hatcheries. Perhaps the best to visit is the **Kosgoda Turtle Hatchery** where (depending on the time of year) you may see leatherback, loggerhead, green, hawksbill and olive Ridley turtles.

The concept behind the hatchery is that the eggs of turtles found by fishermen all along the southwest coast are bought and hatched before being freed into the nearby warm waters of the Indian Ocean – in times past they would simply have been eaten. In this way, over a period of 10 years, an estimated two million young turtles have been 'saved' (although the great majority will still be eaten by carnivorous birds and marine life). The project was badly hit by the 2004 tsunami, but rebuilding is in progress.

Fishing harbour at Beruwela

respectively, these are Sri Lanka's major package tourism resorts, with numerous all-in hotels and every sort of facility. The area is particularly popular with German visitors, and it's not unusual to be addressed in German rather than English by hawkers and hoteliers alike. There's no question that the beach is particularly fine, but it's neither the most reasonably priced nor the most tranquil of destinations on the island. River trips along the wide Bentota River are a popular diversion.

South of Bentota lies a string of fine beaches, including **Aluthgama**, **Induruwa** and **Kosgoda**. These are ideal places for sun, sea and sand, with

Devil's mask at the Mask Museum, Ambalangoda

STILT FISHERMEN

All along the south coast, from Hikkaduwa towards Weligama, long stakes have been driven into the seabed anything from 15 to 150m (16 to 165yds) offshore. Perched on these stakes, like human cormorants, are the stilt fishermen of Sri Lanka. Stilts are passed down from father to son and are therefore highly valued. Each fisherman makes his way out at low tide and returns when the tide has once again fallen, or by boat. The catch, caught by rod, is kept hanging from the top of the stilt. Best viewed either at dawn or at dusk.

Because 26 December 2004 was a Buddhist holy day, no fishermen were working when the tsunami struck.

numerous top- and middle-range places to stay, good local and international food, and plenty of water sports available. The major hotels and dive shops at Aluthgama can arrange diving. The waters are clear and the variety of fish seems endless. In and around Kosgoda turtle hatcheries are a major attraction (*see p77*).

Ambalangoda

Some 86km (54 miles) south of Colombo, the broad, white sweep of beach at Ambalangoda is an attraction in its own right. But Ambalangoda has something the rest of the beach resorts in southwestern Sri Lanka don't have – a sophisticated mask-carving tradition, and two of the best mask museums in the island. The craft shops of the master mask-carvers tend to be concentrated in the north part of town (and, being on higher ground, were protected from the 2004 tsunami, though tragically many

Sinhalese script on an outrigger at Hikkaduwa

of the workers and their homes were swept away). Here, too, are the **Ariyapala Mask Museum** and the **Mask and Puppet Museum**, where masks are also on sale.

Museums. Open: daily 8.30am–5.30pm. Free admission.

Hikkaduwa

Beyond Ambalangoda, and the last stop before Galle, is the enduringly popular beach resort of Hikkaduwa. This was a genuine beachside paradise 20 years ago, but today the charm of the place is severely limited by the main Colombo–Galle Road running right through the heart of town. This is both seriously dangerous and noisy, and until the local authorities get around to building a ring road (or even some speed bumps) the reputation of Hikkaduwa is bound to suffer.

It's still tremendously popular, but as it grows in size, with an accompanying lack of taste and increasing prices, it's bound to lose out to more laid-back destinations further around the coast towards Unawatuna and Tangalle (*see pp88 & 92*). It's still a good place to pass through, but it's no longer paradisiacal by any stretch of the imagination.

The deep south

The ancient port of Galle is Sri Lanka's fourth-largest city, with a population of around 80,000 people and a history that stretches back hundreds of years. Some historians have suggested that Galle might even be the biblical Tarshish, where King Solomon's ships called to take on gemstones, spices and scented woods. There's nothing to establish the truth of this rather fanciful tale, but it is at least certain that Galle is Sri Lanka's oldest living city, contrasting with the more ancient – but deserted – capitals of Sigiriya, Anuradhapura and Polonnaruwa.

Galle

Located on the southwestern shore of the island, about 115km (72 miles) south of Colombo and just 18km (11 miles) south of the popular beach resort of **Hikkaduwa**, Galle was for centuries Sri Lanka's main port, a position which strengthened during the periods of Portuguese and Dutch colonial rule. Galle only lost its primacy in the late 19th century, when the British expanded and developed the harbour at Colombo to become the island's major port. Today Galle Harbour still handles fishing vessels, a certain amount of container traffic, as well as a few luxury yachts. It's a shadow of its former self, though, and this adds to its mellow, laid-back atmosphere.

Although there is plenty of good accommodation available in Galle, as

The southern coast

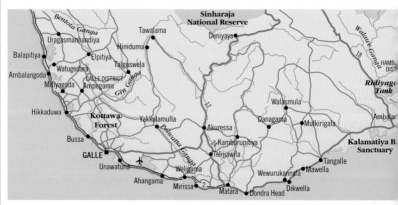

well as some very passable places to eat, many visitors will prefer to stay at one of the nearby beach resorts of **Hikkaduwa**, **Unawatuna** or **Weligama**. A visit to Galle makes an excellent and enjoyable day trip when it seems time to take a break from beach life and indulge in a little history and culture.

History

Galle was clearly chosen as a port for excellent strategic reasons. It has a fine natural harbour protected, to the west, by a south-pointing promontory – the next piece of land to the south is the frozen waste of Antarctica, over 8,000km (5,000 miles) distant.

Perhaps the earliest recorded reference to Galle comes from the great Arab traveller Ibn Battuta, who visited the port in the mid-14th century. The Portuguese first arrived in 1505, when a fleet commanded by Lorenzo de Almeida took shelter from a storm in the lee of the town. Clearly the strategic significance of the harbour impressed

the Portuguese, for 82 years later, in 1587, they seized control of the town from the Sinhala kings and began the construction of Galle Fort. This event marked the beginning of almost four centuries of European domination of the city, resulting in the fascinating hybrid – architecturally, culturally and ethnically – that Galle is today.

The Dutch captured the city from the Portuguese in 1640, and immediately began strengthening the fortifications. They remained for almost 150 years, until the city was in turn taken by the British in 1796. Not until 1948, when Ceylon gained its independence from the British, did Galle become, once again, independent. By this time the long years of association with European colonialism had left an indelible stamp on the city, making it unique in today's Sri Lanka. In recognition of this fact, the Old City of Galle was declared a World Heritage Site in 1988.

New Galle

Galle is really a tale of two cities. Inland, to the north of the Colombo–Matara Road, is the modern commercial area, characterised by a jumble of bustling stores, warehouses and small restaurants. Here, by the banks of the old Dutch Canal, is the railway station, bus station and main bazaar. It's a place to arrive, leave, eat, shop for necessities or change money. The only building worthy of note is **St Mary's Cathedral**, built by the British in 1874, and of more interest for the

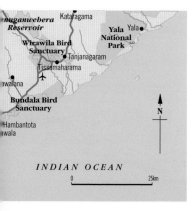

Old Galle *(for walk route see pp86–7)*

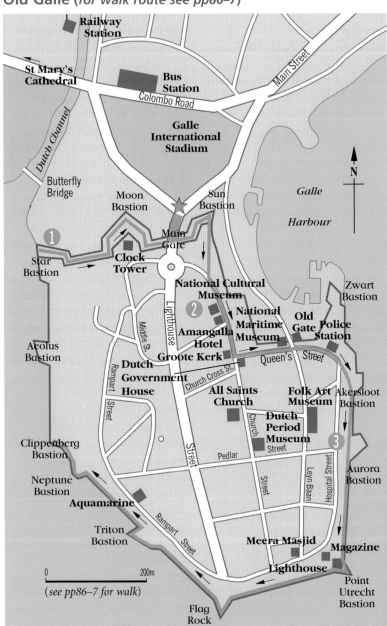

Railway Station

St Mary's Cathedral

Bus Station

Colombo Road

Main Street

Galle International Stadium

Dutch Channel

Butterfly Bridge

Moon Bastion

Sun Bastion

Galle Harbour

N

① Main Gate

Star Bastion

Clock Tower

Lighthouse

National Cultural Museum

②

Zwart Bastion

Amangalla Hotel

National Maritime Museum

Old Gate

Police Station

Aeolus Bastion

Groote Kerk

Dutch Government House

Church Cross St.

Queen's Street

Middle St.

Rampart Street

All Saints Church

Folk Art Museum

Akersloot Bastion

Church Street

Dutch Period Museum

③

Clippenberg Bastion

Neptune Bastion

Street

Pedlar Street

Leyn Baan

Hospital Street

Aurora Bastion

Aquamarine

Triton Bastion

Rampart Street

Meera Masjid

Magazine

Lighthouse

Point Utrecht Bastion

0   200m

(see pp86–7 for walk)

Flag Rock

GALLE CRICKET STADIUM

Cricket is a Sri Lankan national obsession, and what's more the Sri Lankan national team has proved exceptionally good at playing the game. Consequently, in recent years Galle International Stadium has emerged (together with Colombo and Kandy) as one of three main test match grounds in Sri Lanka. Aficionados claim that the pitch at Galle is generally a hard, flat batting track. Also, its proximity to the seashore gives the air a bit of a bite, giving the fast bowlers something to look forward to in the first half an hour or so.

Since Galle became a test venue in 1998 Sri Lanka have won nearly every match they've played at the ground. It would be hard to find an international cricket stadium in a more historic location. Badly damaged by the tsunami, the stadium was rebuilt and opened in 2007.

views it provides over the Old Town than for any intrinsic architectural merit. Nevertheless, 'New Galle' is the beating commercial heart of the city, without which the Old Town would have difficulty surviving. New Galle sustained severe damage in the tsunami disaster and reconstruction is currently in progress.

Immediately south of the Colombo–Matara Road, and dividing the commercial sector from the old fort, lies an area of open land that is graced with the title **Galle International Stadium**, an international test cricket venue, which has witnessed the remarkable successes of the Sri Lankan national team. In 2007 it hosted the third Test of England's tour to Sri Lanka. (*see panel above*).

Old Galle

Just to the south of the stadium, the fortified peninsula of Old Galle begins. Its barriers are unmistakable, as three massive bastions rise up behind the playing field, cutting off the fortified peninsula from the hustle and bustle of commerce – almost, it might seem, from the 21st century.

Old Galle covers an area of 36 hectares (89 acres) and encloses several museums, a clock tower, churches, mosques, a lighthouse and several hundred private dwellings. Tellingly, there are no major Buddhist temples within the walls – the Dutch may have been gone for more than two centuries, but their cultural influence, best represented by the crumbling **Groote Kerk**, local seat of the Dutch Reformed Church, is palpable.

The real charm of Old Galle lies in the quiet back streets and alleyways of this historic fort, which have changed little since colonial times. There are two entries into the fort, the **Main Gate**, built by the British in 1873, which pierces the ramparts between the **Sun and Moon Bastions**, and the more venerable **Old Gate**, further to the east on Baladaksha Maw (or Customs Road). The Old Gate is distinguished by the British coat of arms carved into its outer stone lintel, while on the inside the initials VOC, flanked by two lions and surmounted by a cock, are deeply etched on the inner lintel. This latter inscription is dated 1669, and VOC stands for the

The deep south

The British Church and the lighthouse from Moon Bastion in Galle

Vereenigde Oostindische Compagnie, or (Dutch) United East India Company. The cockerel has become a symbol of Galle, and it has been suggested that the name of the city derives from *galo*, which is 'rooster' in Portuguese. Just beyond the Old Gate stands the **Zwart Bastion**, or Black Fort – the oldest fortification surviving in Galle, and thought to be of Portuguese origin.

With the exception of Zwart Bastion, the interior of Galle Fort is strongly redolent of the Dutch period. Several of the narrow streets still bear Dutch names such as Leyn Baan or 'Rope Lane' and Mohrische Kramer Straat or 'Street of the Moorish Traders'. Beneath the streets an efficient, Dutch-built sewerage system is still flushed out twice daily by the rising tides of the Indian Ocean. Many of the streets are lined with formerly opulent buildings characterised by large rooms, arched verandas and windows protected by heavy, wooden-louvred shutters.

The northern part of the Fort is dominated by the British-built **Clock Tower** and a small roundabout located immediately within the Main Gate. From here Church Street curves away south past the **National Cultural Museum** (*open: Tue–Sat 9am–5pm. Admission charge*) with exhibits of the city's colonial heritage. The **National Maritime Museum** on nearby Queen Street (*open: Tue–Sat 9am–5pm. Admission charge*), housed in a fortified Dutch warehouse, suffered severe tsunami damage but reopened in 2008 with a new first floor gallery focusing on the lifestyles and practices of fishing communities. It's also worth making a quick visit to the **Dutch Period Museum** on Leyn Baan (*open: daily 8.30am– 5.30pm. Free admission*). This privately owned establishment houses an astonishing array of Dutch-period artefacts.

Of more interest than the museums is the dilapidated **Groote Kerk** or Dutch Reformed Church, located on Church Street south of the **Amangalla Hotel**. Founded in 1754 by the then Dutch Governor of Galle, it is well worth visiting for the ancient Dutch gravestones. These are generally distinguished by skulls and skeletons, characteristic of the dour nature of contemporary Dutch Protestantism.

Opposite the Groote Kerk stands the old **Dutch Government House**, a fine old colonial building bearing the date 1683 and the cockerel crest of Galle over the main entrance. The original Dutch ovens still survive within the building, which is generally believed to be haunted.

Further south along Church Street stands the Catholic **All Saints Church**, built by the British in 1868 and consecrated in 1871. Beyond this, a small Moorish community still prospers, with a *madrassa* or Islamic college and two mosques, the most impressive of which is the **Meera Masjid**. It's fine to enter, but you should be appropriately dressed and respectful.

MALDIVIAN TRIBUTE

For many centuries the sultans of the remote Maldive Islands, set in the central Indian Ocean some 500km (300 miles) southwest of Sri Lanka, paid an annual tribute to the Kings of Ceylon through the port of Galle.

This tribute, formally acknowledging Ceylonese suzerainty over the Maldives, was sent to Galle aboard sailing vessels known as *baggala*. These tiny vessels, having made the hazardous crossing from Malé, the Maldivian capital, would bestow gifts of the finest Maldivian mats, beautiful lacquerware, sweetmeats, palm honey, fish paste and small but valuable quantities of ambergris on the Ceylonese kings. By all accounts it was a solemn and picturesque tradition, but the last tribute was sent in 1948, the year in which Sri Lanka gained its independence; the Maldives became an independent republic in 1968.

Walking on Galle promenade, from the lighthouse

Walk: Galle city ramparts

It takes a full day to explore Old Galle properly, but some exploration can be carried out in a leisurely manner by foot. The ancient walls, dating in large part from the Dutch establishment of the fort in 1663, are mostly intact and make a wonderfully evocative walk around the fort, especially at dusk when the setting sun illuminates the western ramparts.

Allow 2–3 hours to explore the walls. See map on p82 for the route.

Start at the war memorial north of the old city and walk south 50m (55yds) to the main gate.

1 The northern bastions

Galle's Dutch defenders feared – mistakenly, as it turned out – assault by land from the Sinhala kings more than the threat by sea from the British.

Accordingly, three great ramparts were built at tremendous cost in both labour and treasure to isolate the peninsula from the mainland. Stretching across the peninsula from west to east, these are the Star Bastion, the Moon Bastion and the Sun Bastion. Rising high above the present-day esplanade, these deep, crenellated fortifications must once

Part of Star Bastion, Galle Fort

Moon Bastion and Clock Tower, Galle Fort

have appeared impregnable to the armies of Kandy and Colombo. Today, however – and let the visitor be forewarned – their angular crevices provide privacy for courting couples rather than security for archers and musketeers. One should approach these outer battlements with discretion for fear of giving offence. Towards dusk there is hardly a recess in the battlements without its pair of cuddling teenagers, often shielded from prying eyes behind a large umbrella!

2 The Amangalla Hotel

It takes about two hours for a leisurely stroll around the walls of the Old City. Only once, between the Aurora Bastion and the Main Gate, is it necessary to descend into the fort itself. Yet this is no great hardship, for nearby is the distinguished Amangalla (formerly New Oriental) Hotel, built by the Dutch in 1684 as a governor's mansion, where cold beer, lime soda and other sustenance is readily available.

3 Eastern and southern bastions

It's best to make a circuit of the walls clockwise, starting at the Amangalla Hotel. From here it's just a short stroll, beneath great, shady rain trees, to the Aurora Bastion. Continue southwards, with fine views over old Galle Harbour to the east, to reach the 20m (66ft) high lighthouse, built by the British in 1934, which dominates Point Utrecht Bastion at the fort's southeastern corner. The walk continues due west, skirting the Indian Ocean past the Triton, Neptune and Clippenberg Bastions.

Beyond Clippenberg, as the fortifications turn due north towards the Star Bastion and the main northern defences, there is a Sri Lankan Army camp at the Aeolus Bastion, which remains off-limits to tourists.

Unawatuna

Southeast of Galle there are a number of lovely, secluded beaches, the first of which is Unawatuna. A wide, curving bay with a beach straight out of Robinson Crusoe, this tiny village is fast developing into a popular resort catering to surfers, snorkellers, divers and sun-worshippers. It's just 5km (3 miles) from Galle, and an ideal place to stay. Unlike Hikkaduwa, there's no busy road through the middle of the settlement, and it's still fairly laid-back.

Weligama

East of Unawatuna, the road hugs the picturesque south coast for 25km (15½ miles) all the way to Weligama or 'Sandy Village'. Although Weligama Bay is indeed lovely, unlike Unawatuna it's a busy fishing village and therefore holds less appeal for tourists. There are good facilities, however, and both scuba-diving and snorkelling are popular. Another alternative is to go dolphin- and shark-watching in an outrigger catamaran – your guesthouse or hotel will have details. Just inland, across the railway line, is the **Kustaraja**, a large 8th-century rock carving thought to represent a 'leper king' who was cured of the dread disease by an exclusive diet of coconut milk.

Mirissa

This tiny village, 4km (2½ miles) beyond Weligama on the Matara Road, is developing as a low-key resort with fine beaches and almost perfect snorkelling

TAPROBANE ISLAND

Close to shore, in the centre of Weligama Bay, is a gorgeous, tiny island, which is privately owned. Once the property of the French Count de Maunay, it is known both as 'Count de Maunay's Island' and 'Taprobane Island', though its real Sinhalese name is in fact Yakinige Duwa, or 'She-Devil's Island'.

In the 1930s de Maunay built his dream house here, and subsequently in the 1950s the American novelist Paul Bowles wrote much of his book *The Spider's House* in the same elegant gingerbread mansion.

Today it functions as a private holiday retreat, which can be leased at a price. A rickety rope and pulley system between the mainland and the island still functions to send over regular supplies of food, newspapers and other necessities.

conditions. There's good surf and the scene is still markedly more tranquil than that at Unawatuna or Hikkaduwa.

Matara

Located at the southern end of the railway line from Colombo, Matara is a medium-sized town of historical interest to visitors, but not really a destination in itself. Instead, stay at nearby Mirissa or Tangalle and take a day trip to Matara to see the elegant little **Star Fort** built by the Dutch in 1763 and still bearing the VOC initials of the Dutch East India Company. Also of interest are the **Dutch Ramparts** built in the 18th century to protect the Dutch administrative buildings and settlement south of town across the Nilwala Ganga. On the ouskirts of Matara, along the road to Dondra

Fishing vessels and palm trees, Weligama Bay

REDOUTE·VAN·ECK

L·I·E·V·E

1·7   0

Dutch Star Fort, Matara

Head, stands the huge and gaudy **Weherehena Temple**, which is impressive in a very kitschy way.

Dondra Head

Just 5km (3 miles) southeast of Matara you come to Dondra Head, the southernmost tip of South Asia and the last piece of terra firma (tiny islands excepted) before the Antarctic. There's an impressive 54m (177ft) high lighthouse, the revolving light of which is easily visible from nearby Matara at night.

Dikwella and Mawella

East of Dondra the long and pristine coast of southern Sri Lanka continues for mile after mile. At Dikwella,

22km (13¹/₂ miles) from Matara, a narrow road leads inland to the nearby **Wewurukannala Vihara**, another gaudy Buddhist temple reminiscent of Weherahena. After another 6km (3¹/₂ miles) the traveller will reach the **Hoo-maniya Blowhole** at Mawella, where the warm waters of the nearby Indian Ocean can be forced 25m (80ft) into the air through underground passages at high tide.

The deep south

Weherahena Temple, near Matara

Outriggers on the beach, Mawella Bay

Tangalle and Hambantota

There's nothing much to do at Tangalle but lie back and enjoy perhaps the most beautiful beach – or series of small beach-coves – in Sri Lanka. Almost 200km (125 miles) from Colombo, this is as quiet and as pristine as the south coast gets, although some of the beaches shelve deeply and it's safer to sunbathe than to swim. Inland about 15km (9^1/$_2$ miles) is the rock temple of **Mulkirigala**, which may date from the 1st century AD. It's the site of Sri Lanka's 'Rosetta Stone' – a series of Pali manuscripts found in the 19th century that provided the key

to translate the *Mahavansa*, the story of Sri Lanka's earliest history.

Somewhere beyond Tangalle, about halfway along the 42km (26-mile) road to Hambantota, the lush scenery of southwestern Sri Lanka gives way to the arid zone of the southeast. The once-busy fishing village of Hambantota, long settled by Sri Lankans of Malay Muslim ancestry, had a long working beach, but this community was all but wiped out in the 2004 tsunami disaster and will take years to recover. Nearby, however, **Bundala Bird Sanctuary** still provides some of the best bird-watching on the island.

Church at Tangalle

Tissamaharama and Kataragama

Beyond Hambantota and somewhat inland are two southern sites which have nothing to do with beaches. **Tissamaharama** is an ancient, bustling, isolated town chiefly visited for its Buddhist relics and for access to **Yala National Park** (*see pp138–9*). 'Tissa' is centred to the south of Tissa Wewa, a huge man-made water tank thought to date from the 3rd century BC. Between the tank and the town stands a tall white *stupa*, the **Kavantissa Dagoba**, dedicated to 2nd-century BC King Kavantissa of Ruhunu, and next to this is a statue of Queen Viharamahadevi, his wife. Two other *dagoba* of significance are the **Santagiri Wehara,** standing just behind the restored Kavantissa *Dagoba*, and the **Yatala Wehera**, built 2,300 years ago by Yatala Tissa, founder of the Ruhunu Kingdom. Tissa is a town of great rain trees and lakes, with cattle wandering freely in the surrounding countryside. It's a long way from anywhere, but if you're visiting either Yala or Kataragama, then it's the best place to stay.

Tissa is unashamedly and unreservedly Buddhist. But **Kataragama**, 15km (9 1/2 miles) to the northeast, is perhaps the most important pilgrimage site in all Sri Lanka, and holy to Buddhist, Hindu and Muslim alike. An extraordinary place to visit, Kataragama – another name of the Hindu God of War, Skanda – must be almost uniquely syncretic, with religious buildings from all three major religions standing side by side and coexisting in apparent harmony.

The main Buddhist shrine is the **Maha Devale**, said to contain the three-pronged lance of Skanda. Nearby shrines are dedicated to the Hindu elephant-headed god Ganesh and to the Buddha. It's not so unusual to find Hindu and Buddhist shrines side by side in South and Southeast Asia, but just 250m (270yds) to the southeast, right next to the **Sivam Kovil** (dedicated to the Hindu God Shiva), stands a rather delicate, small mosque, the **Kataragama Masjid**. Sri Lanka Moors believe that Kataragama is sacred to a Muslim *pir*, or saint, called al-Khidr, the 'Green Man'. Over the centuries (as with Adam's Peak, *see pp114–15*) the various religious groups that revere Kataragama have learned to tolerate each other and even share in the annual pilgrimage, which takes place during the month when Esala falls (*see p29*). As well as the various religious shrines, Kataragama has an interesting **Archaeological Museum** and statues of two early rulers, King Dutugemunu and King Rewa.

Beyond Tissamaharama, National Route 2 leads north to **Buduruvagala** (*see p101*). It's also possible to drive along a smaller, more isolated road through Yala National Park to reach Buduruvagala by way of the small town of Buttala. This will lead you away from the south coast into Uva Province and the southern interior.

රුහුණු මහා කතරගම දේවාලය

The Maha Devale Temple at Kataragama

The southern interior

The southern interior of Sri Lanka is relatively unvisited by travellers, chiefly because it is geographically located between two of the island's main attractions – the magnificent highlands and the unparalleled beauty of the southern coast. Most visitors tend to skirt the area without actually passing through it. Yet this region, comprising all of Sabaragamuwa Province and a large part of Uva Province, is an attraction in its own right, with much to offer the visitor, not least its pristine isolation.

The main town, and capital of Sabaragamuwa, is the gem-mining town of **Ratnapura**. From here there's a 'back door' to Adam's Peak via the Peak Wilderness, as well as the road south to the **Sinharaja National Reserve** (*see map, p100*). Eastwards, two parallel routes cut across gorgeous hill country, much of it given over to tea cultivation, before meeting at the small gem-mining settlement of Balangoda. From here you can drive north into the Central Highlands via the steep road to Haputale (*see p113*), or continue through the lowlands to the ancient Buddhist site at Buduruvagala on the road to Kataragama (*see p94*) or Arugam Bay (*see p130*).

Ratnapura

Ratnapura, meaning 'Jewel City' in Pali, is Sri Lanka's premier gem-mining centre. Located deep in the southern interior, to the east of the Sabaragamuwa Mountains around 100km (62 miles) from Colombo, it

View across town, Ratnapura

dominates the rich agricultural flatlands between Adam's Peak and the Sinharaja National Reserve. All around are verdant rice paddies, while the hills are covered in extensive tea and rubber plantations. But this is not the bounty that makes the town famous; across the country, and indeed across the region, the name Ratnapura is redolent of rubies, sapphires and moonstones, as well as lesser gems such as zircon, garnets, alexandrite and quartz.

Many optimistic Sri Lankans have made their way here through the centuries to pan in the rivers and, above all, to work in the shallow pit mines (see box below). Most never strike it rich, and those who do make a find generally lose most of the profits to Ratnapura's gem-dealers, many of whom are from the famously entrepreneurial Sri Lankan Moorish community.

As befits such a culturally mixed town, Ratnapura has a major Buddhist temple, the **Gnanasiha Tapowana Vihara,** beyond the small **Pompakelle Forest Park** to the east of town, as well as a central Hindu *kovil* and Muslim mosque, both located to the south of Main Street in the eastern quarter. Yet most visitors will come here to see gems rather than cultural monuments. One good place for this is the famous **Gem Market** on Saviya Mawatha, just opposite the central clock tower. Here you can see dozens of deals taking place at any one time, but *caveat emptor* – unless you're a real expert, let the buyer beware! Otherwise check out the various gem museums.

Gem Bureau and Museum

The Gem Bureau and Museum is a private institution where you can buy gems, but also view exhibitions of mining techniques, polishing and jewellery-making.
Pothgul Vihara Mawatha. Open: daily 9am–5pm. Free admission.

Gemological Museum

Similarly, the Gemological Museum is a private institution selling gems, but also with displays of locally made jewellery and a model of a gem-mining pit.
Ehelepola Mawatha. Open: daily 9am–5pm. Free admission.

GEM MINING

Gem mining in Ratnapura is a tough and risky business. Miners search out the seams of gravel known in Sinhalese as *illama*, which is where precious and semi-precious gems are most likely to be found. *Illama* is most likely to occur in river beds or several metres down in paddy fields. Men either pan the rivers or dig narrow but sometimes dangerously deep pits to find these layers of gravel, which are then laboriously hauled to the surface and washed to check for gemstones. Miners work by paraffin or coconut oil lamps in dangerous and unhealthy conditions. When gems are found, they are sold and the profits divided – although not on an equal basis. The financier who provides the initial investment receives the highest percentage, and the lowliest miner with the least experience the lowest percentage. Some do make it rich, but for most miners it's a hard life with minimal returns.

Gem miner, Ratnapura

Ratnapura National Museum

The museum is located in the western part of town and offers exhibitions of prehistoric fossils discovered in nearby gem pits, as well as precious stones and jewellery made from local gems.
Ehelapola Walauwa, Colombo Rd.
Tel: 222 2451. Open: Sat–Thur
9am–5pm. Closed: Fri & public holidays.
Admission charge.

Maha Saman Devale

About 4km (2¹/₂ miles) west of town along Route 8 to Panadura is the Maha Saman Devale, possibly the richest and most impressive Buddhist temple in Sri Lanka, and dedicated to Sri Pada, the sacred footprint of the Buddha on Adam's Peak. Originally dating from the 13th century, it was rebuilt by King Parakramabahu VI in the 16th century. It was vandalised by the Portuguese during their rule over the island, and besides the remains of Portuguese fortifications next to the temple, there's a stone representation of a Portuguese soldier on display.

Sinharaja National Forest Reserve

Sinharaja is the last great area of primary rainforest to survive in Sri Lanka. It straddles the Sabaragamuwa Mountains about 30km (19 miles) south of Ratnapura and is best reached by taking Route 18 southeast as far as Madampe, then turning south onto Route 17, which leads ultimately to Matara and the south coast (*see map, p100*). Located at the heart of the island's wet zone, the park covers nearly

19,000 hectares (47,000 acres) of strictly controlled natural reserve. From the north, it's possible to enter via Delgoda, and from the south via Deniyaya, but from Ratnapura it's also possible to enter via Rakwana, just north of the Butota Pass. Visitors to the park must be accompanied by an accredited guide.

Sinharaja is home to a mass of flora, including giant bamboos and huge canopy trees up to 50m (160ft) high, which shut out much of the sunlight. More than 200 species of tree have been identified as growing here, as well as a great variety of ferns and other flora.

The park is home to leopards, spotted cats, fishing cats and civet cats, as well as sambar, barking deer, wild boar, porcupines and pangolins. There are numerous species of monkey including the Purple-faced Langur, and around 50 species of reptile, including venomous kraits and green pit vipers. More than 150 different species of bird have been identified, and the insect life seems limitless – especially, visitors should be aware, the number of leeches. Use a topical repellent around socks and feet if walking any distance within the reserve.

Sinharaja jungle vines

Tour: Through Sabaragamuwa to Buduruvagala

One of the best drives in Sri Lanka is the long and narrow back road northeast from Ratnapura, via Gallella and Rassagala, to Balangoda. From here you can loop back to Ratnapura on Route 4, continue to the Hill Country by way of Haputale (see p113), or visit Buduruvagala near Wellawaya, where Route 4 meets Route 2. The countryside is splendid and there's very little traffic.

Allow a full day.

1 Adam's Peak

Head east out of Ratnapura on Route 4 and after about 5km (3 miles) take the narrow road north to Gilimale. If you carry on to Palabaddale you reach the 'back door' to Adam's Peak. From this small village you can climb to the summit in around eight hours, taking about six to return. The views are magnificent, but it's a much harder climb than from Dalhousie (*see p114*), and should only be considered if you are really fit.

2 Tea and rubber plantations

Return southwards and pass once again through Gilimale, then turn left (eastwards) towards Gallella. From here it's a switchback-ride across beautiful countryside through miles of tea plantations and rubber plantations. If it's still quite early in the morning, you should see rubber-tappers with their curved tapping knives and black pots for collecting the raw latex. Often, since the day's work starts early for them and the long, silent avenues

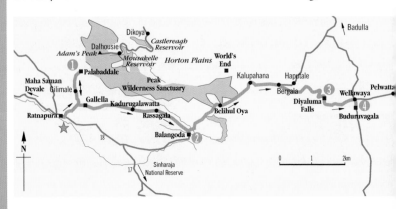

ea plantation workers

of the rubber plantations are dark, they will be wearing flashlights strapped to their foreheads. The tea-pickers, by contrast, work all day. Most are Tamil women, who labour with remarkable dexterity, picking the finest tips of the tea plants and casting them over their shoulder into a collecting bag which hangs there. The road continues through Kadurugalawatta and Rassagala to the gem-mining town of Balangoda, where there are good tea shops selling sandwiches and cakes.

3 Diyaluma Falls
From Balangoda (unless returning to Ratnapura directly via Route 4), head eastwards through Belihul Oya to Bergala, where the road forks. A left-hand turn leads upwards to Haputale and the high hill country around Badulla (*see p111*), but if you continue east along Route 4 towards Wellawaya, you will pass the spectacular 170m (558ft) high Diyaluma Falls. These are particularly impressive during the rainy season.

4 Buduruvagala
At Wellawaya turn south along Route 2 for about 5km (3 miles) watching out for a small side road on your right. About 4km (2¹/₂ miles) along this track is the ancient Buddhist site of Buduruvagala (which means 'stone Buddha images' in Sinhalese). This remote site is thought to date from the 10th century, when Mahayana Buddhism dominated parts of the island. Carved into the rock face is a huge 16m (52ft) high Buddha figure, with three smaller figures on either side. These are thought to represent the Maitreya Buddha, Avalokitesvara and his consort Tara, as well as the Hindu god Vishnu. *Open: daily. Admission charge.*

The flexible bamboo

Bamboo (more properly, 'bamboos', because the botanical subfamily *Bambusoideae* is divided by scientists into more than 75 genera and over 1,000 species) are giant, fast-growing grasses that have woody stems. Indigenous to much of the world, from tropical and subtropical to mild temperate regions, there are species native to the Americas, to Europe and to Africa. But by far the greatest concentration and most spectacular flowering of bamboos is to be found in the Far East and South Asia.

Bamboo is used for scaffolding throughout South and Southeast Asia

Bamboos come in many sizes. The smallest species rise little more than 10–15cm (4–6in) above the ground, whilst the largest – found, invariably, in the warm, wet tropics, like Sinharaja National Reserve (*see pp98–9*) – may attain heights of more than 40m (130ft). Yet they all share certain common characteristics. The hollow, woody stems, known as culms, grow in branching clusters from a thick underground rhizome. Mature bamboos sprout horizontal branches that bear sword-shaped leaves on stalked blades. Though the culms of some species grow quickly (as much as 30cm/1ft a day), most bamboos grow at a more leisurely pace. They flower and produce seeds just once in their lifetime, which may be anything between 10 and 120 years.

The etymological origins of the word 'bamboo' are obscure. Some authorities claim it derives from the Kannada language of South India, and that it is onomatopoeic, representing the crackling, explosive sound made by the culms when they burn. Among the first European references is that of Ralph Fitch, an early English visitor to Southeast Asia, who reported in 1586 that 'all the

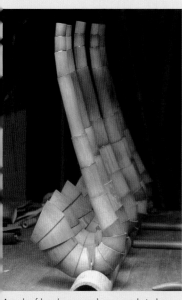

A rack of bamboo saxophones ready to have the mouthpiece fitted

houses are made of canes, which they call bambos, and bee covered with strawe'. Twenty years later the Dutch voyager Linschoten, on a visit to the East, marvelled on seeing 'a thick reede as big as a man's legge, which is called bambus'.

What impressed these early European travellers was not just the ubiquitous nature of bamboos in the tropics – they seemed to be everywhere – but the extraordinary range of uses to which they were put. Even in the 21st century, the uses of bamboo remain immensely diverse. The seeds are eaten as grain, and the cooked young shoots of some species are eaten as vegetables. The raw leaves are used as fodder for livestock. The pulped fibre of several bamboo species is used to make high-quality paper. A fine-grained silica known as *tabasheer*, produced from the joints of bamboo stems, has been used as a medicine in the Orient for centuries. There's no doubt the bamboo is a very useful plant indeed.

But that's not all. Bamboos are beautiful to look at, too, celebrated for centuries by painters and poets. Few people can fail to be moved by the quiet elegance of bamboos in an ornamental garden. Nor will they remain unstirred by the swish and clack of the 40m (130ft) giants of Sinharaja as they sway and bend – but never break – lashed by the sudden violence of a tropical storm.

Bamboo comes in all shapes and sizes

The Central Highlands

The Central Highlands are the tea-growing region par excellence of Sri Lanka. They also offer some of the most magnificent scenery to be found anywhere in the island. The main attraction, beyond doubt, is Nuwara Eliya, the queen of Sri Lanka's hill stations. There's also the pilgrim route to Adam's Peak, Sri Lanka's most sacred mountain, and the extraordinary landscape of the Horton Plains, Sri Lanka's high tableland.

On the Horton Plains the landscape is so reminiscent of a cold northern moor that it's scarcely possible to imagine the idyllic tropic strand of southern Sri Lanka is only 100km (60 miles) distant. At the aptly-named 'World's End' the Horton Plains suddenly fall sharply for more than 1,000m (3,300ft) to the sweltering plains below. Around Nuwara Eliya there are numerous attractions, including **Pidurutalagala**, Sri Lanka's highest peak, and the Hakgala Botanical Gardens. Beyond Nuwara Eliya the hill country continues through carefully tended tea estates to Badulla, the capital of Uva Province.

From here the traveller can either continue east to Arugam Bay (*see p130*), or head south to Buduruvagala and Kataragama (*see p94*). The most fascinating route is to go back through the hill country past Ella and Bandarawela to the charming tea-estate town of Haputale, the northern gateway to Sabaragamuwa and the southern interior (*see p113*).

Kitulgala

Within about 50km (30 miles) of bustling Colombo, as you head east along Route 4 to Avissawella and the Berendi Kovil, the road begins to rise sharply through Kegalla District, passing through the small settlement of Kitulgala. It was here that the film-maker David Lean made his 1957 Oscar-winning epic *Bridge on the River Kwai*, and those familiar with the film will be able to recognise some of the settings. Nowadays Kitulgala is also known for its white-water rafting on the **Kelaniya Ganga** (Lean's substitute for the real River Kwai in Thailand). Arrangements can be made through the local Rest House or the nearby **Plantation Hotel** (*Kalukohutenna. Tel: 228 7575*).

Hatton, Dikoya and Dalhousie

Beyond Kitulgala, Route 7 continues to climb beside the mountain railway line through to the rather shabby market town of Hatton. There's nothing in

Hatton itself to attract the traveller, yet it's the junction for pilgrims visiting Adam's Peak (*see pp114–15*). If the sacred mountain is your destination, take the small side road south to Dikoya and continue via Maskeliya to the small town of Dalhousie, the main starting point for the 7km (4¹/₂-mile) climb to Sri Pada, the summit of Adam's Peak. (The summit is also accessible by a far more difficult route from the south via Ratnapura, *see p100*.)

Kotagala

Beyond Hatton, Route 7 continues eastwards, winding through lovely mountain country past tea estates to the small town of Kotagala. This is the heart of the Dimbula Tea District, and it's a good place to stop and visit a tea estate. A good option is **Christler's Farm Estate** (*www.wilstea.com/christlersfarm.htm*), producer of Robert Wilson's Ceylon Teas, which is well set up for visitors (they'll try to sell you

some tea, naturally – slogan 'a whiff of morning mist'). Also near Kotagala are the magnificent **St Clair's Falls**, in fact a double cascade flowing from the Kotmale Oya. The larger fall, Maha Ella, is 80m (262ft) high and the smaller, Kuda Ella, 50m (164ft) high. Together, they plunge through three cascades into a deep pool, producing clouds of vapour, especially during the rainy season.

Nuwara Eliya

Beyond Kotagala the road continues to climb through **Talawakele** and **Nanu Oya** (the railway station for Nuwara Eliya) before arriving in the famous hill station itself. Nuwara Eliya – often shortened to Nurelia and meaning 'city of lights' – is situated 1,890m (6,200ft) above sea level, making it Sri Lanka's highest town. As such it is blessed with a temperate, invigorating climate. Situated on a plateau measuring 6.5km (4 miles) by 2.5km (1¹/₂ miles), it is

The Central Highlands

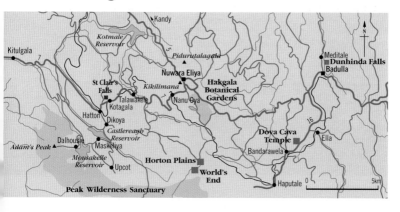

ringed by hills and mountains which appeal to hikers, trekkers and naturalists. The town itself is small enough to explore on foot within a few hours. All around, there are sloping tea plantations, some stretching right into the outskirts of town. To add to these attractions, the numerous British-style country houses scattered about town give Nuwara Eliya an attractive, albeit quaint, colonial feel.

Nuwara Eliya was 'discovered' in 1826 by a group of British officers who had lost their way while on an elephant hunt. In those times Nuwara Eliya was a nondescript little village surrounded by thick jungle. This was rapidly to change. The officers informed the British governor of Ceylon, Sir Edward Barnes, of their find, and he soon made his way to Nuwara Eliya to investigate in person.

SIR SAMUEL BAKER

Sir Samuel Baker, the famous British explorer of the Nile, visited Nuwara Eliya in 1847 to recuperate from an attack of malaria. He was so taken by the setting that he decided to settle there 'and build a little English town around my residence'. Baker returned a year later with seeds, tools, cows, sheep, a horse and pack of foxhounds. He moved on after eight years, leaving behind a healthy flock of sheep, a herd of cows, and flourishing acres of potato fields, as well as other temperate vegetables and a number of 'neat white cottages'. Baker eventually died at his Devonshire family estate in 1893. He left for posterity two books describing his time in Nuwara Eliya, *The Rifle and Hound in Ceylon* (1853) and *Eight Years in Ceylon* (1855). Though he did not found 'The City of Lights', he contributed substantially to its prosperity.

Recognising its potential as a health resort, Barnes built himself a residence

The Grand Hotel in Nuwara Eliya

there in 1828. Soon after, he initiated the construction of a sanatorium. In next to no time, the healthy and invigorating reputation of Nuwara Eliya began to spread across the island, and sickly or homesick Europeans began to move in. By 1859 the hill station had developed such a positive reputation that the visiting naturalist Sir J E Tennent was to write that 'in the eyes of the European and the invalid, Nuwara Eliya is the Elysium of Ceylon'.

To facilitate travel to Nuwara Eliya, Barnes ordered a road built from Kandy, 77km (48 miles) away, which was already well connected with the capital Colombo. This highway, today's Route 5, is an alternative way of reaching Nuwara Eliya, and passes through truly spectacular hill country, through well-tended tea estates and deep gorges, with fine views across the **Kotmale Reservoir** near Ramboda. At its eastern end, the road was continued to Badulla. Thus well connected, Nuwara Eliya grew by leaps and bounds. Holidaying colonial officers were simply delighted with Nuwara Eliya's climate – 'so reminiscent of home' – and many built houses that would not have seemed out of place in Sussex or Kent.

To provide entertainment, a racecourse was established in 1875, while in 1889 a golf course followed suit. In 1900, several hundred prisoners from the Boer War in South Africa were employed to build **Victoria Park**. Though somewhat neglected, it remains the central feature of the town today. In 1911, Ceylon's first brewery was founded in Nuwara Eliya, making use of the crystal-clear and pure water of the region to produce 'Lion Beer'. The climate also proved ideal for growing temperate-climate vegetables such as carrots, cabbages, beans, tomatoes and potatoes, as well as strawberries and even roses.

Today, Nuwara Eliya has lost hardly any of its charm. Most visitors come to enjoy the clean, cool air, soak up the quaint colonial atmosphere and visit the numerous tea estates. Aside from the tea plantations, tourists can also visit some tea factories in the area. One factory open to visitors is **Labookellie**, 10km (6 miles) along the Nuwara Eliya–Kandy Road. You can also purchase some of Labookellie's tea, which is supposed to be among Sri Lanka's best. The tea estate is also an easy taxi ride from Nuwara Eliya.

Terraced vegetable gardens, Nuwara Eliya

Sri Lanka's Tamil tea pickers

The tea gardens around Nuwara Eliya make a superb subject for photography, especially when there are scores of sari-clad Tamil tea-pickers in them – from a distance they may appear like giant locusts munching their way through the greenery. Yet, the tourist's joy is somebody else's pain. Work on the tea estates is hard and badly paid (less than US$2 per day); on many days there is no work (and no pay) at all. To get to the plantations, many women have to walk two or three hours across the sloping hillsides. Given their meagre income, it is hardly surprising that some of the women ask for a few rupees from camera-toting tourists. There are

Hauptale makes an ideal base for visiting tea plantations

some fair-trade tea gardens in the area, such as the Venture Estate and the Stockholm Tea Estate.

The tea pickers are almost without exception Tamils, who make up around 18 per cent of Sri Lanka's population (see pp22–3). Properly speaking, they should be referred to as 'Indian Tamils', as opposed to the Tamils living in the north and northeast of the country, who are called 'Ceylonese Tamils' or 'Jaffna Tamils'. The Indian Tamils are descendants of plantation workers whom the British brought over from Tamil Nadu in Southern India in the 19th and early 20th centuries. The Ceylonese Tamils on the other hand claim descent from Tamil warrior dynasties, who invaded Sri Lanka for the first time in 237 BC. In the following centuries, Sri Lanka was invaded, and even sometimes ruled, by Indian Tamils, laying the foundation for an enduring hostility between the Tamils and the Sinhalese.

In the early 1960s, the government of Srimavo Bandaranaike decided to 'repatriate' 525,000 Indian Tamils to India, who – based on a controversial citizenship law of 1949 – were considered stateless. Another 300,000 stateless Indian Tamils were allowed

A tea plantation near Nuwara Eliya

to remain. The repatriation was met with strong resistance and thousands of deportees hid from the authorities. In the end, many of them succeeded in staying put.

Yet not everything is as it should be even within the Tamil community itself. Despite their common roots, many Ceylonese Tamils tend to look down upon their later-arrived, and mostly poor, Indian Tamil brethren. Both groups speak Tamil, but in slightly differing dialects. The Ceylon Tamils outnumber the Indian Tamils by about two to one. As for their religion, about two thirds of the Tamils in Sri Lanka are Hindus, the remainder Christians and Muslims.

Muthiyangana Vihara, Badulla

only men – until 1965, women were only allowed in through the back door! When the club was finally on the verge of bankruptcy, it was converted into a hotel. Even today, though, the Hill Club has retained much of its old-time snobbishness: guests are required to dress 'decently' at all times, and after 7pm gentlemen must sport jackets and ties in all public areas of the hotel, while ladies should wear evening gowns or similar formal dress. Come 5pm in Nuwara Eliya, the sun will rapidly disappear behind the mountains and the air will quickly get chillier. Put on warmer layers, ask the hotel staff to light the fire in your room, have a tea and sit back and enjoy. They don't make places like this any more.

Around Nuwara Eliya

There are a number of interesting excursions in the vicinity of Nuwara Eliya. **Shantipura** or 'City of Peace' is a small village situated 4km (2¹/₂ miles) west of Nuwara Eliya. Take a bus from Nuwara Eliya's minibus station. North of the village you see the mountain **Kikilimana** (2,238m/7,343ft), which can be climbed with some effort but without any special equipment. Also nearby is **Pidurutalagala**, Sri Lanka's highest mountain (2,524m/8,281ft), which rises just north of town. You can trek along its lower reaches, but as there is an army camp further up you are unlikely to be allowed anywhere near the peak. A third pleasant and easy destination within easy striking

In Nuwara Eliya, just spending time in the hotel can be sheer bliss. Aside from numerous middle-class guesthouses, the town boasts several first-class, mansion-type hotels, with cosy colonial-style rooms and lush, well-tended gardens. One such place is the **Grand Hotel** (*www.tangerinehotels.com/thegrandhotel*), opened in 1891 and built in rustic Tudor style. Despite its old-world charm (including rustic fireplaces in the rooms), you will also find a shopping arcade, billiards and table-tennis rooms and a tennis court.

The most tradition-bound of Nuwara Eliya's hotels is the **Hill Club**. As its name implies, it was originally conceived as a club, founded in 1858 to cater for British colonial officers and coffee planters. In line with other such establishments, the Hill Club admitted distance of Nuwara Eliya is **Hakgala Botanical Gardens**. Originally an experimental plantation for nutmeg, cardamom and cinchona, an important source for the anti-malarial drug quinine, today these delightful gardens are home to many exotic trees, flowers and other plants. The gardens are situated just 10km (6 miles) southeast of town, on the road to Badulla.

Horton Plains and World's End
Situated 2,150m (7,054ft) above sea level, **Horton Plains** may remind British visitors of Dartmoor or the Scottish Highlands. Cool, sharp winds hiss over a steppe-like, grassy and rather bleak landscape. In the evenings you may see dozens of sambar deer. At **World's End** (4km/2½ miles away), the plateau drops abruptly by 1,650m (5,413ft) and allows spectacular views – in very clear weather to as far as the coast. To get to Horton Plains, rent a jeep or car at

Nuwara Eliya. It's a fine day trip, but should be avoided in rainy or very cold weather.

Badulla
The old tea-planters' town of Badulla is the end of the line, at least as far as the Central Highlands are concerned. There's little enough to see in town itself, although there is adequate accommodation and it's an ideal spot to overnight if you are touring in this area. Badulla Train Station is the end of the Colombo–Kandy hill country railway line, and there's a Methodist church to remind the visitor of the town's past links with the British. North of town are the spectacular **Dunhinda Falls**. About 5km (3 miles) along the road to Meditale, this 60m (200ft) high cataract crashing through the jungle makes a good picnic spot, and is especially impressive after the rains. *Admission charge.*

A reservoir at Horton Plains

Ella Rock towers over the small town of Ella

Ella

This picturesque little town, situated at 1,100m (3,609ft) and surrounded by lush greenery, is famed for the view from **Ella Rock**, a massive outcrop at the very edge of the hill country looming 1,000m (3,280ft) above the coastal plains. On a clear night it's possible to make out the light of **Kirinda Lighthouse**, almost 100km (62 miles) distant.

Near Ella one of the most extraordinary engineering feats of 19th-century railway construction can be seen in the '**Ella Loop**', where the track performs a full loop before disappearing beneath itself through a mountain en route to Badulla. Because

of this, and the magnificent scenery in general, one particularly enjoyable way to get to Ella is to take the train from **Nanu Oya** near Nuwara Eliya (around 50km/31 miles). Ella has long been a popular retreat, and excellent accommodation is available.

Bandarawela

Route 16 south from Badulla leads past Ella to the small hill resort of Bandarawela, a busy market town with a substantial Tamil and Moorish population, which is both attractive and well provided with facilities – accommodation, banks, post office, petrol station, a branch of Cargills department store, and a neat little station on the Colombo–Badulla mountain railway. It's well known for its prosperous Sunday market, and makes an excellent base for exploring the surrounding countryside. Other attractions include the well-known **Suwa Madhu Ayurvedic Treatment Centre**, and the Dowa temple about 6km (3¹/₂ miles) east of town, where an elegant 4m (13ft) high standing Buddha has been cut into the rock face.

Haputale

This attractive, predominantly Tamil and Muslim town straddles a very high ridge between Bandarawela and the southern lowlands towards Buduruvagala (*see p101*). It's a pleasant little place, with fantastic views and good access to Ella, Horton Plains and World's End. It's in the heart of the tea country, and was once home to Sir Thomas Lipton of Lipton's Tea fame. Visitors can still view his Haputale factory, built in 1890 and now called **Dambatenne Tea Factory**, located about 11km (7 miles) out of town. **Lipton's Seat**, a viewpoint by the factory, is said by some to have views that rival World's End.
Dambatenne Tea Factory. Open: daily except Sun. Admission charge.

Hill country with lush vegetation at Bandarawela

Walk: Adam's Peak

This is a place to test your physical fitness: Adam's Peak is Sri Lanka's fourth-highest mountain (2,243m/7,359ft) and the country's holiest pilgrimage site. On the peak, you will find an oversized 'Buddha Footprint', but non-Buddhists also revere the mountain. The ascent should ideally be started at about 1 or 1.30am, so as to arrive in time for sunrise. In clear weather, this is a truly spectacular sight from the peak.

1 Dalhousie

If you don't have your own transport, take a bus from Nuwara Eliya to the twin towns of Hatton and Dikoya and change on to a bus for Dalhousie. There the 7km (4$^1/_2$-mile) long trail begins, zigzagging up over 1,000m (3,280ft).

2 The route to the summit

If you decide to make the ascent during the pilgrimage season, be aware that the entire route will be packed with throngs of pilgrims. There are tea houses where

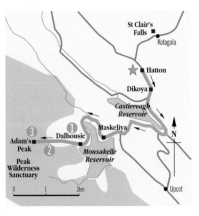

you can sit and take refreshments every few hundred metres all the way to the top, and the pathway and seemingly endless steps are illuminated, making quite a sight as you look back. On the other hand, if you make the climb out of season there will be far fewer people, but most of the tea houses will be closed, so take some refreshments with you. The path isn't illuminated between June and November, so a torch is also a necessity. It's cold on the summit, Sri Pada, at night, so warm clothing is essential, and a flask or two of hot tea is also a good idea. But if all this sounds difficult, it will certainly seem worth it when you watch the sun rise from the east, casting (in the right weather conditions) a near-perfect shadow of the summit of Adam's Peak on the mist-filled valleys to the west.

3 The sacred footprint

Adam's Peak is sacred to all of the island's main faiths. There is a strange indentation set in the living rock of the

Mist-shrouded Adam's Peak from the south

summit. To the majority Sinhalese Buddhists (74 per cent of the total population) it is the footprint of the Gautama Buddha. The Tamil Hindus (18 per cent) know better – it is, of course, the sacred footprint of the god Shiva. Then again, the island's Muslims (7 per cent) insist it is the footprint left by Adam when, cast out of the Garden of Eden by a wrathful God, he fell to earth in the place nearest to that celestial grove in terms of beauty, fertility and climate, Sri Lanka. For centuries Sri Lanka's Buddhists, Hindus and Muslims – together with many of the island's Christians, who agree with the Muslims that the footprint is indeed that of Adam – have been content to disagree amicably and share the pilgrimage season, which runs from December to May every year. Every night thousands of people climb the seemingly endless stairs to the 2,243m (7,359ft) summit and await the sunrise.

The Cultural Triangle

In recent years north-central Sri Lanka has been much promoted by the Sri Lanka Tourist Board as 'the Cultural Triangle' – and with good reason. While the south coast offers some of the most beautiful beaches on earth, the roughly triangular area encompassing Kandy (see p60), Anuradhapura and Polonnaruwa is home to some of the richest and most impressive archaeological monuments in Asia.

Just north of Kandy, on Route 9 to Matale, is the ancient rock temple of Aluvihara. The road continues north past the 8th-century Nalanda Gedige temple to the rock temple of Dambulla. At this point Route 6 heads east towards the stunning rock fortress of Sigiriya, surely a high point in any exploration of Sri Lanka's history, and on via Route 11 to the ancient capital of Polonnaruwa.

Meanwhile, Route 9 continues northwest from Dambulla to another ancient capital, Anuradhapura, and to the two-millennia-old Buddhist centre at Mihintale. Just off Route 9, on the way to Anuradhapura, is the elegant 5th-century Aukana Buddha, while Route 28 from Anuradhapura to Kurunegala leads past the 13th-century rock fortress of Yapahuwa. The whole region is rich in museums and must be considered an archaeologist's paradise. It's also very beautiful, and home to a wide variety of wildlife.

One advantage of Sri Lanka's promotion of the 'Cultural Triangle' as a tourist attraction is that the Central Cultural Fund of the Ministry of Cultural Affairs issues a single ticket permitting entry to seven major sites in the region, namely Anuradhapura,

CULTURAL VOCABULARY

Bodhi Tree Also known as the Pipal, the species of tree (*Ficus religiosa*) under which the Buddha attained enlightenment.

Chedi, Chetiya Buddhist shrine.

Dagoba see **Stupa**.

Kovil Hindu temple.

Lingam Phallic symbol of Shiva.

Mahayana The 'greater vehicle', Buddhism as practised mainly in Japan, China and Vietnam (as opposed to the Theravada, see below).

Pokuna Tank or artificial pond.

Poya Full moon holiday.

Sangha A community of Buddhist monks.

Stupa Buddhist monument, usually hemispherical, containing a relic of the Buddha or Buddhist holy man.

Theravada The 'way of the elders', the oldest form of Buddhism, as practised in Sri Lanka.

Vatadage Circular relic house.

Vel Trident, the weapon of Skanda.

Vihara A sacred Buddhist complex.

Dambulla Museum, Polonnaruwa, Sigiriya, Nalanda, Ritigala and Medirigiriya.
Ministry of Cultural Affairs, 21 2/1 Bauddhaloka Mawatha, Colombo 7. Tel: 250 0732.

Aluvihara

The rock monastery of Aluvihara stands just east of Route 9 about 3km (1³/₄ miles) north of Matale. The name – which means 'ash temple' – derives from a legend that in times past a giant

The Cultural Triangle

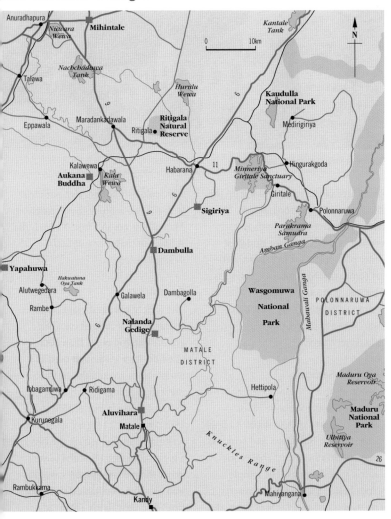

Entrance to the Dambulla Caves

used three of the rocks making up the site as a rest for his cooking pot. The temple is extremely ancient, as a council of the Sangha, or Buddhist order of monks, was held here in the 1st century BC to transcribe Pali texts. The tradition survives, and visitors can see monks writing holy texts on ola palm leaves at the temple today. *Admission charge.*

Nalanda Gedige

The 8th-century Nalanda Gedige is to the east of Route 9, about 22km (14 miles) north of Aluvihara. A temple sacred to both Buddhists and Hindus, it has some rather weathered erotic Tantric rock carvings. The temple stands beside a large tank or reservoir. The style is unusual for Sri Lanka, and

archaeologists have drawn parallels with the 7th-century shore temple at Mamallapuram in Tamil Nadu, India. *Admission charge or Cultural Triangle ticket.*

Dambulla

The rock temple and giant Buddha at Dambulla is centred on a huge granite outcrop more than 500m (1,640ft) high. Although used as a temple from around the 1st century BC, the wall paintings for which the temple is famous date from the 15th to the 18th centuries. There are several large reclining Buddhas within the caves, and a gigantic modern Buddha towers above them. Five separate caves have wall paintings, on subjects ranging from Buddhist (both Theravada and

Mahayana traditions – *see box, p116*) to Hindu, as images of Vishnu and Ganesh may also be found. Nearby, Dambulla Museum offers interesting exhibits on rock and wall paintings. *Open: daily 8am–5.30pm. Admission charge or Cultural Triangle ticket.*

Sigiriya

The single most impressive ancient monument in Sri Lanka is surely the ancient rock fortress of Sigiriya. This outcrop rises abruptly from the surrounding plains of north-central Sri Lanka, dominating the country for miles around. A massive monolith of red stone, so sheer that the top overhangs the vertical walls on all four sides, it looms 349m (1,145ft) above sea level and 180m (591ft) above the surrounding scrub and jungle.

All but impregnable to surprise attack and even sustained siege, there are indications that the great rock was first inhabited by aboriginal hunters more than two millennia ago. It was not until the 5th century AD, however, that Sigiriya entered briefly into a golden age as the seat of Sinhalese power in medieval Sri Lanka. The story surrounding this blossoming has been described by the historian Zeylanicus as 'a barbaric tale of vindictive passion, romantic beauty and superhuman endeavour without parallel in the bloodstained annals of Lanka'. Certainly, as this lovely, tear-shaped island is still threatened by a

The ancient rock fortress of Sigiriya at sunset

bloody civil war so many centuries later, it bears relating again.

In AD 459 Dhatusena, a Sinhalese of noble birth, defeated his Tamil rivals and established a new capital at Anuradhapura in Sri Lanka's northwest. His eldest son, Kasyapa, was born soon after to a minor queen. Subsequently the chief queen bore him another son, Mogallana, who was held to be the legitimate heir by virtue of his mother's superior rank. Needless to say, this sat badly with Kasyapa, who seized the throne by force in 477 and walled up his father alive. Meanwhile, Mogallana, fearing for his life, fled into exile in the Tamil realm of south India.

Thereafter Kasyapa is said to have felt remorse for his ruthless deed, though it is equally probable his actions were driven by fear of his brother's return. Whatever the case, almost as soon as he had seized the throne by patricide he began fortifying the massive outcrop at Sigiriya, building a splendid palace atop the great megalith. Here he ruled for eleven years. Even today it is easy to imagine him, sitting on the smooth stone known as the king's throne, admiring the elaborate gardens constructed on the plain below while simultaneously scanning the horizon uneasily for his brother.

The lower steps at Sigiriya

The lion's paws at Sigiriya

His fears proved far from groundless. In 495 Mogallana, backed by Tamil forces, returned in search of revenge. Unwisely, Kasyapa descended from his lofty perch to meet the invaders, directing the advance of his soldiers from elephantback. Soon the great beast became separated from the bulk of the army and Kasyapa, isolated and in despair, committed suicide by stabbing himself in the throat. Flushed with victory, Mogallana proclaimed himself king and transferred the capital back to Anuradhapura, leaving the rock fortress of Sigiriya to the wild beasts, the jungle and an obscure order of cave-dwelling monks.

Climbing Sigiriya offers wonderful views across the countryside, and the visitor can relax on the summit amid the shattered remnants of Kasyapa's palace. The climb isn't easy, however, and even if you are fit you should allow 2–3 hours to make the ascent.
Open: daily 7am–6pm. Admission charge or Cultural Triangle ticket.

Walk: Polonnaruwa

About 35km (22 miles) east of Sigiriya, just off Route 11 linking Anuradhapura and Batticaloa, lies the sleepy provincial capital of Polonnaruwa, 215km (134 miles) distant from bustling Colombo. It's difficult to imagine now, but between the 10th and 13th centuries AD Polonnaruwa was the splendid capital of Sri Lanka.

This walk takes in the main sights of Polonnaruwa. Allow 4–5 hours.

1 Parakrama Samudra

Unlike Anuradhapura, where the remnants of past glory are spread over an extensive area, in Polonnaruwa they are relatively easily accessible on foot or by bicycle. The most obvious legacy of the old kingdom is the Parakrama Samudra at the western rim of town. King Parakramabahu I (1153–86) ordered the building of the colossal tank both for water storage and as a defensive barrier. A 3.5m (11ft) high statue near the southern end of the tank supposedly portrays Parakramabahu and conveys a deep notion of dignity and nobility; the figure is rendered with great artistic economy and restraint. About 200m (220yds) south of the statue, Parakramabahu built the Potgul Vihara or 'Library-Monastery'. Besides a library, the building encompassed a mysterious, round and domed building fortified with walls 3m (10ft) thick. *Head north on New Town Rd.*

2 The citadel

The core of Polonnaruwa's old city is the citadel near the Parakrama Wewa, which was originally surrounded by a wall. The citadel encompasses the remnants of what is usually regarded as Parakramabahu's palace. Though almost completely in ruins, the remains

---

Map labels:

Gal Vihara — 8 — The Rock Monastery
The Alahana Pirivena Group — 7
Lankatilaka
6
Ruvaneli Dagoba — Satmahal Prasada
5
Great Quadrangle — 4
Kumara Pokuna — King's Council Chamber — Audience Hall
3
Royal Baths — 2
The citadel
1st Chanel Rd
Batticaloa Rd
New Town Rd
N
0   500m
1
Parakrama Samudra
Potgul Vihara

give a good idea of the labyrinth of rooms the palace must have contained. Holes in a remaining wall indicate where wooden beams were affixed, possibly to support a wooden balustrade. The palace included a Great Hall which in all likelihood included a throne for the monarch and seating arrangements for the audience. Here, the king took his decisions, reputedly with the help of a multi-racial council consisting of four Sinhalese, four Muslims, four Christians and four Jews. If true, King Parakramabahu must have been one of the most tolerant and enlightened rulers of his time.

3 The Kumara Pokuna

Southwest lies the Kumara Pokuna or 'Princely Pond', a royal bath-tank which once was flanked by two lion figures. The water flowed through taps shaped like crocodile heads.

4 Great Quadrangle

North of the citadel, the most important remains of the old city are spread out. As in Anuradhapura, hardly any of the secular buildings have survived. The most interesting collection of ruins is found in a relatively small area north of the citadel, often referred to as the Great Quadrangle. Its most attractive edifice is the Vatadage or 'Round Relic-House'. This is based on two overlying round platforms, the upper slightly smaller than the lower, which were surrounded by a wall. At the cardinal points, gates and staircases interrupt the wall. Each staircase leads up to the figure of a seated Buddha, and the four Buddhas gaze serenely in the four cardinal directions. The staircases are ornamented in great detail, with moonstones laid out at their bases, arches depicting *makaras*, mythical sea-crocodiles, as well as flower ornaments, guardian-stones, lions, dwarfs and other decorative motifs. Immediately to the north stands the Thuparama, a walled temple with a curved roof.

5 Satmahal Prasada

The Satmahal Prasada, built by Nissanka Malla, is an interesting reminder of the communications that Sri Lankan monks maintained with Southeast Asia. The pyramid-like structure had seven levels (now reduced by time to six), becoming consecutively smaller towards the top. Quite unlike any other structure in Sri Lanka, it bears a striking resemblance to two 13th-century *stupas* at Lamphun in northern Thailand, then the Kingdom of Haripunchai, with which Sri Lanka maintained close religious ties.

One of the Buddhas at the Vatadage

6 The Ruvaneli Dagoba

This huge *dagoba*, also known as the Rankot Dagoba, stands further north, and with a height of 55m (180ft) is the highest *dagoba* in Polonnaruwa and the fourth highest in Sri Lanka. Its circumference is 165m (541ft).

7 The Alahana Pirivena Group

Still further north, an assortment of buildings was erected within the precinct of the cremation grounds for the members of the royal family and senior members of the Sangha or council; the buildings are collectively known as the Alahana Pirivena Group. The small *stupas* scattered over the area are thought to be tombs. The most striking edifice in the group is the Lankatilaka Image House (also called Jetavanarama), a large temple lined by 18m (59ft) high walls. Its outside is decorated with numerous bas-reliefs. At the western end inside the Lankatilaka, at the far side of the entrance, there is a 13m (43ft) high figure of a standing Buddha, made of brickwork and originally coated with stucco.

8 The Rock Monastery

From here, a path leads north, first through some minor ruins, then in between two tanks to Polonnaruwa's most striking architectural monument: the Gal Vihara or 'Rock Monastery'. The Gal Vihara was part of an extensive sacral complex credited to Parakramabahu I, called Uttararama or 'Northern Monastery', comprising four

Polonnaruwa: Standing Buddha at Gal Vihara

massive figures hewn out of a horizontal escarpment of streaked granite rock. The figures depict the Buddha in his three main poses of sitting, standing and lying; each figure was originally covered by its own image-house. A male figure, 7m (23ft) high, stands left of the recumbent Buddha's head. His arms are crossed and he wears a somewhat less beatific, even slightly morose expression on his face. It is sometimes assumed that this figure represents Buddha's devoted disciple and cousin Ananda, as he mourns the death of his beloved teacher. The crossed arms, however, might indicate that the figure portrays the Buddha himself, since he was occasionally depicted in this manner, for example in a painting in the Dambulla Caves (*see pp118–19*). *Admission charge or Cultural Triangle ticket.*

The rediscovery of Sigiriya

Sigiriya remained forgotten for almost 1,500 years until 1831, when a Major Forbes of the Indian Army reported the 'rediscovery' of the great rock during the course of his explorations, although an ascent to the long-abandoned summit was too dangerous to contemplate.

Sigiriya soon began to attract a small flow of curious Western visitors, including the Buddhist scholar T W Rhys Davids, who in 1875 was startled to see half-hidden frescoes of beautiful women when scanning the rock with his telescope (see The Cloud Maidens, *pp14–15*). Who had painted these images – and, indeed, how, since they were concealed beneath a giddy overhang halfway up the precipitous west face – remained

H C P Bell, the first Archaeological Commissioner for Ceylon

a mystery until 1889 when Alick Murray, a British engineer on service in Sri Lanka, went to extraordinary lengths to reach them.

In 1895 the great rock came under the investigation of H C P Bell, the first Archaeological Commissioner for Ceylon. Bell's pioneering work soon suggested that the solitary megalith was Kasyapa's long-lost fortress, a conclusion put beyond doubt when in 1898 he uncovered two enormous stone lion paws on a platform halfway up the sheer north face.

Under Bell and his successors the work of excavation proceeded apace. A narrow, precipitous path leading to the Lion Platform was cleared, and a 3m (10ft) high wall erected by Kasyapa as a balustrade was exposed. This structure, coated with an incredibly smooth glaze and incised with hundreds of age-old graffiti, is known as the 'Mirror Wall'. Far above it the gorgeous frescoes remained tantalisingly out of reach until October 1938, when the Archaeological Commission of Ceylon erected a vertiginous spiral staircase to the overhang, making the maidens accessible to the general public for the first time ever.

Medirigiriya

Located in arid country about 30km (19 miles) north of Polonnaruwa, Medirigiriya is famous for the Mandalagiri Vihara, a *vatadage* or relic-house similar to the better-known one at Polonnaruwa, but far more isolated and therefore quieter. Thought to date from the 2nd century AD, it stands on a low hill. Four Buddha images face in the cardinal directions around the central *dagoba*.
Admission charge or Cultural Triangle ticket.

Ritigala

In the Ritigala Nature Reserve close to Route 11 between Anuradhapura and Habarana, Ritigala is the site of an ancient forest monastery thought to date from the 4th century BC but abandoned seven centuries later following Chola invasions from

MIHINTALE

The important site of Mihintale lies around 12km (7¹/₂ miles) east of Anuradhapura on Route 12 to Trincomalee. This ancient centre is of great spiritual significance to Sri Lankan Buddhists, as it was here, in 247 BC, that King Devanampiya Tissa of Anuradhapura was converted to Buddhism by Mahinda.

Mihintale is located on top of a huge granite outcrop and is approached by a series of flights of stairs – 1,840 steps in total, so it's quite a climb. On the way up the visitor passes a ruined hospital and the Kantaka Chetiya dating from around 240 BC, but the real attraction at Mihintale is the summit. Here two whitewashed *dagobas*, the Ambasthale Dagoba and the Mahaseya Dagoba, jostle for space with craning coconut palms and granite outcrops. The views are inspiring, and there's a small museum with frescoes, pottery fragments and bronze figurines on display.
Admission charge.

neighbouring India. Today extensive but deserted ruins remain scattered

Mihintale *dagoba* and giant Buddha

across an arid hill. There is also a complex of caves once inhabited by forest monks.

Admission charge or Cultural Triangle ticket.

Anuradhapura

The north-central city of Anuradhapura first became Sri Lanka's capital in 380 BC, and it remained so for around 1,000 years. Today it's effectively two towns – the modern city, which is a well laid-out, shaded and pleasant town, and the ancient city, which lies a little distance to the northwest. It's a much more spread-out place than Polonnaruwa, and you'll need to use taxis or perhaps hire a bike if you're feeling energetic.

Modern Anuradhapura is surrounded by three of its oldest and most vital structures, the reservoirs or 'tanks'. **Tissa Wewa** and **Basawakkulama Wewa** flank the city on the western side, and **Nuwara Wewa** stretches along its eastern side. The reservoirs are probably the edifices least affected by the ravages of time. Right in the centre of the old town stands the **Sri Maha Bodhi** or **Sacred Bo Tree** (*see pp32–3*), which, after the Buddha's tooth in Kandy, is the most revered Buddhist symbol in the country. After his conversion to Buddhism, King Devanampiya Tissa asked Emperor Ashoka of India for a branch from the Bo tree in India under which Siddhartha Gautama had attained enlightenment. Ashoka complied and sent a sapling from the

Bo tree, which was duly planted in Anuradhapura. Today, the Bo tree in Anuradhapura is the oldest documented tree in the world. With more than 22 centuries to its credit, it still looks in the prime of health. A platform has been built around it, accessible by a stone stairway. At the bottom of the stairs, there is a golden figure depicting the delivery of the hallowed sapling. Pilgrims pay their respects to this figure, then they climb up the stairs to pray at the Bo tree itself.

Located in the vicinity of the Sacred Bo Tree, the remains of the **Brazen Palace** or **Loha Prasada** are one of the most enigmatic sites in Anuradhapura. All that is left today of a once exalted and magnificent building are 1,600 grey, monolithic pillars, set up in 40 parallel lines with 40 pillars in each line. Some of the pillars were haphazardly turned upside down or removed from their original site during restoration work in the early 20th century. The Brazen Palace was originally built by King Devanampiya Tissa (250–210 BC) to accommodate the Indian entourage bringing the Bo tree sapling.

Anuradhapura's *dagobas*, spread far and wide over the old city, are the most conspicuous remainders of the glorious past. The construction of *dagobas* reached an early zenith in the Anuradhapura period, and the ones here are among the most notable in the country, or, for that matter, anywhere in the Buddhist world. The 100m (328ft) high **Abhayagiri Dagoba**, or 'Dagoba of the Mountain of Fearlessness', was built by King Valagamabahu in 89 BC, just after he had regained his capital from Indian invaders. The massive, whitewashed **Ruvanveliseya Dagoba** also measures 100m (328ft) in height but is even older than the Abhayagiri Dagoba. The construction was initiated by King Dutthagamani (161–137 BC), but it was still unfinished on his death. His brother and successor Saddhatissa (137–119 BC) completed the work.

The oldest *dagoba* in Anuradhapura, indeed on the whole island, is thought to be the **Thuparama Dagoba**, located a little north of the Ruvanveliseya Dagoba. With a height of only 19m (62ft), it may be one of the smaller religious edifices in Anuradhapura, yet its small size belies its importance. The Thuparama Dagoba was erected by Devanampiya Tissa to mark his

Thuparama Dagoba

conversion to Buddhism in 249 BC. The right collar bone of the Buddha and the plate from which he used to take his meals are said to be enshrined in its interior, both objects being invaluable gifts from the Indian Emperor Ashoka. These Buddha relics endowed the Thuparama *Dagoba* with extraordinary sanctity, and it duly remains a major place of pilgrimage. The Thuparama *Dagoba* is bell-shaped and surrounded by four concentric circles of stone pillars. Flights of stairs at the cardinal points lead up to the circumambulatory walk, the stairs being flanked by well-executed guard-stones.

Although not endowed with the latter's sanctity, the **Jetavana Dagoba** at the northern rim of the old city is Sri Lanka's largest *dagoba*. Its diameter is 112m (367ft) and its height around 120m (394ft). It was built by King Mahasena (AD 274–301).

South of the Sacred Bo Tree and immediately east of the Tissa Wewa, the **Issaramuniya Vihara** is a spectacular rock monastery with several buildings located outside the caves. In a small museum by the cave entrance, some finely executed bas-reliefs are exhibited, which are considered the best in Anuradhapura. Some reliefs portray the royal families of various periods. The most celebrated is 'The Lovers' (*c*. 4th/5th century), which according to different interpretations depicts either a warrior and his beloved or a divine couple. The relief is executed in the Indian Gupta style. Though the

The monumental stairway at Yapahuwa

agobas that the kings erected have survived in some form or other until the present day, the same cannot be said of the royal residences. There are some remains of the palaces of King Mahasena (301–328) and King Vijayabahu I (1055–1110). A beautiful moonstone, formerly placed in front of Mahasena's palace, attracts busloads of tourists today, but otherwise there are no remains whatsoever of any royal splendour or grandeur.
Admission charge or Cultural Triangle ticket.

Aukana Buddha

Difficult to access by road, but just a short walk from Aukana Station on the Colombo to Trincomalee railway line, the magnificent 12m (39ft) high Aukana Buddha is thought to date from the 5th century AD. Hewn from the solid rock (it is still joined at the back to the cliff behind it), this is perhaps the most elegant Buddha image in Sri Lanka. The Buddha is carved in the *ashiva mudra* pose, signifying blessing. Aukana means 'sun eating', and the best time to visit or photograph the image is at sunrise. If you have your own transport, leave Route 9 (Dambulla to Anuradhapura) at Kekirawa and drive along narrow country roads to Aukana via Kalawewa, a distance of around 11km (7 miles).
Admission charge.

Yapahuwa

The ancient rock fortress of Yapahuwa is similar to, but smaller than, Sigiriya. Dating from the 13th century, it was the capital and main stronghold of King Bhuvanekabahu I, who was resisting invasions from south India. Today a steep ornamental stairway leads up to a platform that once supported a temple which is thought to have served as a temporary repository for the holy tooth relic, now at the Temple of the Tooth in Kandy (*see p62*). There are some fine bas-relief carvings and the view from the platform is magnificent. Like Aukana, Yapahuwa is difficult to access unless you have your own transport. It's 4km (2¹/₂ miles) from Maho railway station on the Colombo–Anuradhapura line, or can be reached by car from Route 28 between Kurunegalla and Anuradhapura.
Admission charge.

The east coast

Sri Lanka's eastern seaboard comprises more than 300km (186 miles) of the most gorgeous scenery anywhere in the Indian Ocean. Arugam Bay provides the best surfing in the country and has some of the most peaceful beaches. From Yala in the south to Batticaloa in the centre, the human population is thinly scattered and wildlife thrives. It should be a paradise for locals and visitors alike, but heavy fighting between the LTTE and government forces has put the area completely off-limits for visitors.

The LTTE (*see pp142–3*) claim the coast as far south as Arugam Bay and Pottuvil as part of 'Tamil Eelam'. The situation on the ground has sadly deteriorated and the visitor must treat the entire area with caution. The British Foreign Office is advising against all travel to the north and east of the country, and to Yala National Park and the areas around it.

Arugam Bay and Pottuvil

Arugam Bay is a small and picturesque fishing village just about as far from anywhere as you can get in Sri Lanka, even on the sparsely populated east coast. The nearest small town, Pottuvil, is about 4km (2½ miles) to the north across a shallow and attractive lagoon. There's a long stretch of palm-lined beach, which offers good swimming for most of the year.

Because of its isolation and the civil war to the north, Arugam Bay was off-limits for years but, following the 2002 ceasefire, the Pottuvil–Arugam Bay area developed into something of a tourist hotspot on the east coast. The main reason for this, apart from the natural beauty and tranquillity of the area, is surfing, but always check the latest security situation before travelling. The waters off Arugam Bay offer the best surfing in Sri Lanka, especially during the peak season between April and September. The water is consistently warm, so no wet suits are needed. The best surfing spots are **Pottuvil Point** to the north, and **Crocodile Rock** and **Peanut Farm** to the south. Arugam Bay was fast turning into a surfer's paradise, with a commensurate growth in accommodation, but is currently closed.

The predominantly Moorish town of Pottuvil just north of Arugam Bay has little to offer the visitor, but just outside town the ancient ruin of **Mudu Maha Vihara** or 'great temple by the sea' shelters a 3m (10ft) high standing Buddha and two smaller figures of the Bodhisattva Avalokitesvara. The temple is in a poor state of preservation and is threatened by advancing sands.

Another popular attraction is **Pottuvil Lagoon**, and ecotours by boat can be arranged through local hotels once the area has opened up again. For two relaxing and fascinating hours you will be paddled through a complex of mangrove swamps and sandbars. There's bird life aplenty, as well as sea creatures and wild animals of many species including, sometimes, elephants. Proceeds from these tours are used in mangrove reforestation projects run by the local Fisheries Cooperative Society.

One of the most interesting ruined archaeological sites on the island, **Magul Maha Vihara**, is located 12km (7½ miles) inland from Pottuvil on the long and isolated road to Badulla. It is attributed to King Dhatusena (AD 459–477), father of Kasyapa, who built Sigiriya. Within a small area there are monuments in several distinctive styles. Guard-stones and moonstones are in particular abundance and variety. Parts of the complex are believed to be 2,000 years old, others perhaps considerably younger. At the entrance is a monk's residence, and on the eastern flank is a crumbling *dagoba*. The four entrances are well preserved, and each is flanked by seated stone lions. The *vatadage*, also well preserved, is in the shape of a fence of plain slabs. A little further south are the remains of a circular

The east coast

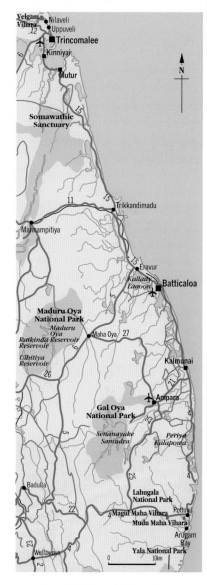

structure with dressed slabs of stone thought to have been used as an elephant stable.

The Ceylon Moors

There have been Muslims in Sri Lanka for well over 1,000 years. Trading dhows plied the waters between the Middle East and the island known to Arab sailors as Serendib even in pre-Islamic times. The first Muslim merchants and sailors may have landed on its shores during Mohammed's lifetime. By the 10th century this predominantly Arab community had grown influential enough to control the trade of the southwestern ports, whilst the Sinhalese kings generally employed Muslim ministers to direct the state's commercial affairs. In 1157 the king of the neighbouring Maldive Islands was converted to Islam, and in 1238 an embassy to Egypt sent by King Bhuvaneka Bahu I was headed by Sri Lankan Muslims.

Muslim-owned fishing vessel

From about 1350 onwards the predominantly Arab strain in Sri Lankan Islam began to change as Tamil Muslims from neighbouring South India moved to the island in increasing numbers. By the late 15th century, when Portuguese vessels first arrived in the Indian Ocean, Sri Lanka's Muslims were truly indigenous to the island, representing a mixture of Sinhalese, Arab and Tamil blood, and speaking Tamil with Arabic overtones, sometimes known as 'Tamil-Arabic'. None of this made any difference to the newly-arrived Portuguese, for whom all Muslims were 'Moors', the name given to their traditional enemies in Morocco and southern Spain. The name Moro – employed as a derogatory designation by the Portuguese – stuck, and is 'worn with pride' by Sri Lankan Muslims, in much the same way as the 'Moros' of the southern Philippines.

In Sri Lanka, as everywhere they went, the Portuguese made a special point of persecuting Muslims. As a consequence, many fled the western littoral which had passed under Portuguese control, and settled in the north and east of the island

Mosque at Haputale

where their descendants live to the present day. A hundred years later, in 1656, when the Dutch replaced the Portuguese, a third element was added to the island's Muslim population, the Malays. Malay sailors had been visiting Sri Lanka for centuries using long-distance outrigger canoes; now, with the arrival of the Dutch, many more were brought from Java to serve their Dutch colonial rulers in Sri Lanka. In time they were absorbed into the island's ethnically diverse Muslim community, although even now many Sri Lankan Muslims identifying themselves as 'Malays' rather than 'Moors' can be found living in Western Province, and especially in Colombo.

Today Sri Lanka's Muslims live scattered throughout the island, from Galle in the south to the Tamil-dominated Jaffna peninsula in the north. Generally they are involved in commerce, from running local stores to dominating the gem business associated with Ratnapura, the 'Jewel City', and much of the capital's import-export business.

Batticaloa

Batticaloa is both an ancient and an attractive town. The oldest Dutch settlement on the island, dating from 1602, it's surrounded by extensive lagoons and has an attractive small Dutch fort dating from 1682 – the VOC (Verenigde Oost-Indische Compagnie) initials of the Dutch East India Company are still visible above the gate. 'Batti', as it is affectionately known, has a large percentage of Tamils and Moors amongst its population and has seen some fierce fighting in the civil war. The Colombo government recaptured the town from the LTTE in 1991, but as recently as 2006 heavy fighting between the LTTE and government forces has

SINGING FISH

Batticaloa is famous throughout Sri Lanka for a strange and puzzling phenomenon, the 'singing fish' of Kallady Lagoon. If you go to the Kallady Bridge (also known as the Lady Manning Bridge) on a still night, preferably full moon, a clearly discernible musical sound, sweet but not loud, can be heard rising from the waters. The locals insist it is the sound of fish singing, and indeed a singing fish is the emblem of Batticaloa City and District. The phenomenon, which occurs most regularly between April and September, has been recorded and broadcast on Sri Lankan radio, but it still isn't clear exactly what causes it. Some say it comes from gafftopsail catfish which congregate in the lagoon on moonlit nights, others that it is the sound of tidal water passing through mollusc shells and rolling pebbles. To experience the 'singing' at its most audible, place an oar in the water and press your ear against the wooden shaft.

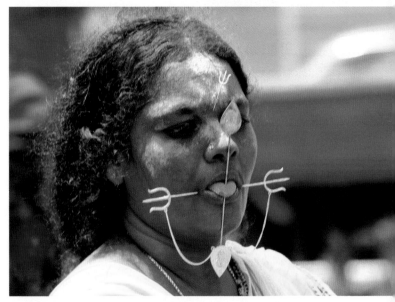

A Tamil woman on the annual pilgrimage between Jaffna and Batticaloa

Fish drying in Pottuvil

Buffaloes and egrets near Trincomalee

put the area off-limits. It's a great pity, as Batticaloa is a bucolic and friendly little town – but nowadays it would be very unwise to go there.

THE JAPANESE AT TRINCOMALEE

Many World War II naval battles took place in the Pacific, but in April 1942, a powerful Japanese naval squadron under Admiral Nagumo, the commander of the Pearl Harbor attack, sailed into the Indian Ocean with the intention of repeating his success at the Royal Naval base of Trincomalee. By good fortune on 8 April Nagumo's force was spotted by an RAF reconnaissance plane that had taken off from Koggala. Forewarned, the Colombo authorities were able to prepare limited defensive measures with the woefully inadequate forces at their disposal. Deprived of the element of surprise, the Japanese decided against landing at Trincomalee, but on 14 April a force of approximately 100 Japanese planes bombed the port, destroying fuel tanks and starting fires that burned for a week.

Trincomalee

Trincomalee is the largest city on Sri Lanka's east coast and also the finest harbour in the whole island. As such, it was a major base for the British Indian Ocean fleet during World War II, and is today the main base for the Sri Lankan navy. There are fine beaches and hotels to the north, but heavy fighting in the harbour in 2006 has made the area off-limits. **Fort Frederick**, originally founded by the Portuguese, is now a military camp, and if Trincomalee opens up you can visit **Koneswaram Kovil** and **Swami Rock** on the peninsula beyond.

About 5km (3 miles) north of town there's a carefully maintained **Commonwealth War Cemetery**, and 10km (6 miles) northwest of Trinco, just off the road to Nilaveli, the 2nd-century **Velgam Vihara** is an isolated

Buddhist complex with some fine examples of Chola temple mouldings.

Nilaveli and Uppuveli

These pristine, crisp white beaches are probably the finest on the east coast, with good opportunities for diving and snorkelling at **Pigeon Island**. New resorts began to spring up as a result of the 2002 ceasefire, but these areas are very close to the main LTTE base area at Mulaittivu, and are unlikely to attract large numbers of visitors until a full peace agreement has been signed.

Hindu iconography on the roof of a Trincomalee *kovil*

Tour: Yala National Park

Yala is the largest national park in the country and is divided into two sections, Yala Park West (Ruhuna) and Yala Park East. Of the two, Ruhuna is the best developed and easiest to visit. Fortunately the largest wildlife inhabits the inland areas of the park and was unaffected by the 2004 tsunami.

Allow one whole day.

1 Palatupana

The gateway to Yala West is the small settlement of Palatupana, about 20km (12^1/$_2$ miles) east of Tissamaharama. Most visitors will make arrangements through a tour company or safari operator, though it is also possible to drive yourself if you have a 4WD vehicle. Park security is taken seriously, and a tracker (who will expect a tip) must accompany all visitors to the park.

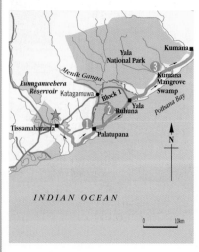

2 Ruhuna

The park is divided into five blocks, and most visitors will restrict their visit to Block 1, south of the Menik Ganga River which flows through the park. Block 1 has one of the densest leopard populations in Asia, and there's a good chance of seeing *Panthera pardus kotiya*, a leopard species unique to Sri Lanka. Other wildlife to watch out for include elephants, sambar deer, spotted deer, sloth bears, wild buffaloes, wild boar, crocodiles and several species of monkey. Yala West is also home to a lot of bird life – around 150 different species have been identified.

3 Yala East and Kumana Mangrove Swamp

Your tracker or safari guide will advise on the best areas to visit and the route to follow, but a narrow road runs close by the coast from Palatupana (where you must buy entry tickets) to Yala town near the mouth of the Menik Ganga. It may also be possible to visit

Yala East National Park by way of Okanda, about 30km (19 miles) south of Arugam Bay, if the road is open. The main attraction here is the Kumana Mangrove Swamp, home to a plethora of bird life.

Open: mid-Oct–Aug, 6.30am–6.30pm. Admission charge.

The British Foreign Office (*www.fco.gov.uk*) currently advises against all travel to Yala National Park and the areas around it following a number of serious security incidents. Visits should only be attempted once the all-clear has been given to resume travel to the region.

Tour: Yala National Park

Leopards are still found in Yala National Park

The north

For around two decades the northernmost part of Sri Lanka has been all but cut off from the rest of the island. At the time of writing, route 9 to Jaffna is closed and it remains largely unsafe; few travellers should risk visiting the area at present. The north can be divided into two main areas: the arid Wanni, a vast area of scrubland between Vavuniya and Elephant Pass, which is dominated by guerrillas of the LTTE (see pp142–3) and the fertile Jaffna Peninsula and offshore islands, which remain contested by the LTTE and the Sri Lankan Army (SLA).

The Jaffna Peninsula

Even in times of peace, the Wanni has little to interest the visitor. Jaffna is another matter, however. An ancient town, for centuries the seat of a Hindu Tamil kingdom quite distinct from the rest of Ceylon, Jaffna thrived as a commercial centre under Tamil, Portuguese, Dutch and finally British rule, retaining its prosperity and distinctive Hindu-Tamil cultural identity.

Until about 25 years ago the main attraction was Jaffna Fort, perhaps once the finest surviving example of a Dutch fort in Asia, but now badly damaged. Dutch influence is also obvious in the **Groote Kerk**, dating from 1706.

The most important Hindu monument in town is the **Nallur Kandaswamy Kovil**, just one of many Hindu temples in town. Jaffna is famous for its markets, and these are now beginning to be rebuilt. The city suffered serious damage during the civil war, however, and it may be years before it returns to its full pre-war prosperity.

ADAM'S BRIDGE

Stretching between Sri Lanka's arid Mannar Island and the nearby coast of Tamil Nadu is a chain of tiny reefs, sandbanks and islets that almost seem to connect India and Sri Lanka. Indeed, in legend they are the stepping-stones of the gods, known as Adam's Bridge, and in the Hindu epic *Ramayana* the monkey-god Hanuman used them to bound to the island to rescue Rama's beloved bride Sita from Ravana, the demon king of Lanka.

Historically there has never actually been a bridge here, but for many decades the venerable, Glasgow-built TSS *Ramanujam* ferried passengers between Talaimannar on the northern tip of Mannar Island and Ramewsaram in Tamil Nadu. That service was suspended in 1984 as a consequence of the civil war, but may well start again if the peace process is successful.

Offshore islands

Just as the Jaffna Peninsula is virtually an island, joined to the mainland by a causeway at **Elephant Pass**, so a number of smaller offshore islands are joined to Jaffna by a series of causeways. The largest of these islands is **Kayts**, distinguished by numerous Roman Catholic shrines. Near the causeway between **Karativu** and Kayts stands a former Dutch fortress called **Hammenhiel Fort**, now a Sri Lankan naval base. Further west and accessible only by boat is the small island of **Nainativu**, home to an important Hindu temple, **Naga Pooshani Amman Kovil**, and also to a revered Buddhist sanctuary, **Nagadipa Temple**. Finally, the most isolated of the offshore islands, **Delft**, was named after the ceramic-producing town in Holland. There's a small Dutch fort and – yet another sign of the island's past association with the Dutch – locally bred Delft ponies introduced from the Low Countries many centuries ago.

The north

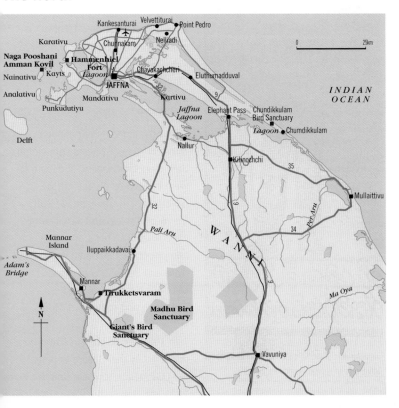

The Tamil Tigers

For some now inexplicable reason, the military thinkers of the British Raj classified the Tamil population of their vast empire as a 'non-martial race'. It's clear that the average Tamil

Government recruiting poster, Badulla

would prefer to live at peace and do business – something at which Tamils excel. They are also some of the friendliest and most hospitable people in South Asia. But there's nothing 'non-martial' about the much-feared Liberation Tigers of Tamil Eelam (LTTE) or their steely commander, Velupillai Prabhakharan.

For many years there have been fierce rivalries between the majority Sinhalese and minority Tamil populations of Sri Lanka, and after independence relations deteriorated rapidly, with serious communal rioting directed against Tamils in 1958, 1977 and 1981. By the early 1980s the independent-minded Tamils of the north were demanding their own state, Eelam, and many were in open revolt against the government in Colombo. By 1985 the most ruthless and hard-line of various Tamil factions, the LTTE, had physically eliminated its local rivals and begun a campaign of ethnic cleansing against Sinhalese, and sometimes Moors, in the north.

In 1987 the Sri Lankan authorities, dismayed by their failure to defeat the LTTE, requested help from New

LTTE leader Velupillai Prabhakharan signing the ceasefire agreement in 2002

estimated 25,000 men, and both women and children were pressed into service as fighters. By 2000 it was clear that neither side could win an outright victory, and Sri Lanka's appeal as a tourist destination was shattered. This was compounded in July 2001, when the LTTE, in a daring night attack, destroyed most of the Air Lanka fleet on the ground at Katunayake Airport.

Seemingly nothing would make ruthless Velupillai Prabhakharan compromise. Then, just a few months later, on 11 September 2001, Al-Qaeda staged its devastating terror attacks on New York and Washington. The USA responded by announcing a worldwide war on terrorism, and seemingly Prabhakharan saw the writing on the wall. A ceasefire was agreed between the government and the LTTE in 2002 and peace talks continued, mainly under Norwegian mediation. The LTTE renounced their demand for an independent state, but continue to demand autonomy for much of the north and east of the island. Escalating violence in these areas from 2006 to 2008 left hundreds of people dead and thousands homeless, while attacks in Colombo continue to make headlines. In 2008 the ceasefire was broken, raising new fears for any lasting peace.

Delhi, and an Indian Peace-Keeping Force (IPKF) was sent in to help disarm the rebels. The move was resisted by the LTTE, and over the next three years Prabhakharan's guerrillas gradually wore down the morale of the world's fourth-largest army, killing more than 1,000 Indian soldiers. In 1990 the IPKF withdrew, and in 1991 a female LTTE suicide bomber assassinated the Indian premier, Rajiv Gandhi. By the mid-1990s much of the north was back under LTTE control, but the region was devastated and Sri Lanka was fast approaching national bankruptcy. During the fighting the LTTE lost an

Getting away from it all

Despite a civil war which has put large tracts of Sri Lanka out of bounds for almost two decades, and renewed violence from 2006 to 2008 between the LTTE and government forces, this lovely Indian Ocean island has much to offer, both in terms of protected wildlife reserves and wilderness trekking. There's also white-water rafting at Kitulgala (see p104) and water sports. There are also three beautiful botanical gardens, most notably at Peradeniya.

For information about parks and nature reserves across Sri Lanka, contact the Department of Wildlife Conservation, *382 New Kandy Road, Malambe, Colombo. Tel: 256 0380. Fax: 274 4299. www.dwlc.lk*

SRI LANKA'S WILDLIFE

The most interesting species of Sri Lanka's fauna inhabit the country's nature reserves, which make up about ten per cent of the land area. With a bit of luck, visitors can still see wild boar, bears, crocodiles, deer, peacocks, wild buffaloes, jackals, giant monitor lizards, 450 species of birds, 95 species of snakes (six of them venomous) and several species of monkeys. There are also still a few leopards, but sightings are very rare. Since man-eating leopards were a regular feature of village life for ages, the big cats have never been very popular with the locals. At the opposite end of the popularity scale are the elephants, which on one hand are cherished for their intelligence, and on the other hand are regarded as a symbol of the Buddha. In the late 1990s there were still 3,500–4,000 elephants in Sri Lanka, however today it is closer to 2,000.

National Parks and Nature Reserves

Gal Oya National Park

This huge national park, covering almost 63,000 hectares (155,676 acres), is situated in the northern reaches of Uva Province, a long way from anywhere (*see map, p41*). It's centred on the Senanayake Samudra, one of the largest reservoirs in the country, and is home to many wild elephants. It's carefully protected by the Wildlife Department in Colombo, which maintains bungalow accommodation in the park. Entrance to Gal Oya is via the small settlement of Inginiyagala, but at present the area is considered unsafe for visitors.

Horton Plains National Park

This windswept moorland is home to sambar deer. *See p111.*

Kaudulla National Park

Centred on Kaudulla Tank, close to Medirigiriya (*see map, p117*), this is Sri Lanka's newest national park and wild elephants are the major attraction. There are also leopards, sloth bears and civet cats. The park is easy to visit, being just 15km (9¹/₂ miles) east of Ritigala on Route 6 between Dambulla and Trincomalee.

Kottawa Conservation Forest

Located in the south of the country not too far from Galle (*see map, pp80–81*), this small park is centred on a 15-hectare (37-acre) wetland evergreen forest, like a miniature Sinharaja National Reserve. There's the same problem with leeches, too, so use insect repellent and wear stout socks and shoes. Several well-maintained trails crisscross the forest. Fifteen kilometres (9¹/₂ miles) northeast of Galle, this is an easy park to access, but get permission from the Forest Department near the entrance before entering.

Lahugala National Park

One of the major attractions in the remote Arugam Bay area, this small park (around 1,500 hectares/3,700 acres) is renowned for the variety of its bird life and its wild elephants (*see map, p131*). However, the area around the park is not currently safe to visit – check with the Foreign Office (*www.fco.gov.uk*) before travelling. Eventually Lahugala should make a superb side trip from Arugam Bay. Head east from Pottuvil past the Magul Maha Vihara (*see p131*), about 16km (10 miles) along Route 4 to Buttala.

Minneriya Giritale Sanctuary

Another sanctuary centred on an ancient tank that provides water and greenery for the wildlife (*see map, p117*). Just over 8,800 hectares (21,750 acres) in area, the park is home to wild elephants, sambar deer, leopards and troops of macaque monkeys. There's also an astonishing range of bird life, including flamingos, painted storks and cormorants. Minneriya is easy to get to. Just head east for about 18km (11 miles) along Route 11 from Habarama to Vandeloos Bay. Tickets must be bought at Ambagaswewa between Habarama and the park entrance.

It's still possible to see leopards in Kaudulla National Park

Peradeniya Botanical Gardens

Sinharaja National Forest Reserve
See pp98–9.

Tangamalai
This tiny nature reserve and bird
sanctuary is situated in the hill country
near Haputale. There aren't any large
mammals like elephants to be seen, but
according to bird enthusiasts in nearby
Haputale (*see p113*) a profusion of
brightly coloured birds can be seen.
Head west out of Haputale along Temple
Road for about 3km (1³/₄ miles). It's an
easy and pleasant walk. There seem to be
no entrance formalities or admission
charge – it's all very relaxed.

Uda Walawe National Park
This large park centred on the Uda
Walawe Reservoir covers an area of
31,000 hectares (76,600 acres) and is
justly famed for its wild elephants (*see
map, p41*). Indeed, it may be the best
national park to visit in the island. As well
as herds of elephants, the visitor can hope
to see leopards, sambar deer and herds of
wild buffalo. Smaller animals such as
bandicoots, foxes, monitor lizards,
crocodiles and sloth bears also abound.
About 35 different species of bird life
have been identified. The park is
unusually well set up, with a hotel, a
'wildlife safari village', bungalows and
campsites. Contact the Wildlife
Department in Colombo for further
details and reservations. Uda Walawe is
best approached from Embilipitiya on
Route 18 inland from Ambalangoda to
Ratnapura. Most people will prefer to
make arrangements for a tour through
their hotel or an agency.

Wilpattu National Park
See p73.

Bird-watching Reserves
Bundala Bird Sanctuary
A flat, coastal region of saltpans and
wetlands, this is home to around 150
different species of bird, as well as a
variety of wildlife, from elephants to
crocodiles, civet cats to turtles. Bundala
lies to the east of Hambantota (*see p92
and map, p81*). The entrance is at
Weligatta, but most tours are organised
in and leave from Hambantota. There are
two authorised campsites in the park.

Kalamatiya Bird Sanctuary
About halfway between Tangalle and
Hambantota, Kalamatiya Lagoon is being
developed into a protected bird sanctuary
(*see map, p80*). Many visitors also arrange
tours in this area to look for turtles.
At present there is little structured
organisation by the Wildlife Department.
Ask at any tour shop in Tangalle.

Wirawila Wewa Bird Sanctuary

A huge and ancient reservoir near Tissamaharama (*see map, p81*) has been made into a protected bird sanctuary by the Sri Lankan authorities. A causeway runs across the wetlands from Wirawila town towards another broad expanse of water, the Tissa Wewa (*see p94*). Bird-watchers can stroll across the causeway for an hour or two, ideally in the early morning or late evening. At present, as at Kalamatiya, there is little in the way of bureaucratic structure at Wirawila Wewa. Make your own arrangements at Tissamaharama.

Marine National Park
Hikkaduwa Marine National Park

The only marine national park in Sri Lanka, and truth to tell, it's something of a disappointment (*see map, p71*).

Tourists in large numbers don't make for good preservation, and the once beautiful coral reefs at Hikkaduwa have been badly degraded. Nevertheless, there are still fish and reefs – sometimes even turtles – to be seen, and glass-bottomed boat trips are a regular feature of visits to Hikkaduwa. Several of the large hotels organise snorkelling, diving and glass-bottomed boat tours, as do virtually any of the many dive shops in town.

Botanical Gardens
Hakgala Botanical Gardens
See pp110–11.

Henaratgoda Botanical Gardens
See p76.

Peradeniya Botanical Gardens
See p67.

Sea Turtle Conservation, Kosgoda

Shopping

It may be the intricate stone carvings in the Ancient Cities, fashioned by craftsmen from the distant past, that attract visitors to Sri Lanka. Yet once in the country, few can resist buying a work by one of the country's contemporary craftspeople that are displayed to such good effect in the country's many shopping outlets. Perhaps the most striking souvenirs are the colourful masks, but there is a wide variety of other woodcarvings. Besides these traditional crafts, Sri Lanka is famous for its gems, teas and spices.

One of the great temptations for Western visitors when looking around the gift shops is that prices are so cheap that it seems a crime not to go home with a bag full of bargains. Going on a shopping spree for low-cost goods can be fun, but visitors need to be on the lookout for fakes, particularly when buying gems or designer clothes. The Ceylon Tourist Board can provide a list of reputable retailers, particularly for gems.

WHAT TO BUY
Clothing
Sri Lanka is a major centre for the production of garments, and some of the designer brands that have their clothes made here include GAP, Ralph Lauren and Next. Most are exported to Western countries, but they are also sold in Sri Lankan boutiques and malls at temptingly low prices. It is possible to pick up a well-made shirt for as little as Rs1,000 or a sari for under Rs3,000.

It is thus an excellent idea to fit yourself out with a new set of clothes while in the country, but caution is necessary when buying, as fake products abound.

Gems
It is fitting that this jewel of an island should be one of the world's major sources of precious gems. Blue sapphires, rubies, amethysts, topaz, moonstones and more are to be found here, so it is hardly surprising that these items feature on many visitors' shopping lists. Ratnapura (*see pp96–8*) is the centre of gem mining and trading, though if you are considering a purchase, it is worth contacting the Sri Lanka Gem & Jewellery Exchange (*see listings*), which provides a certificate of authenticity with each item. Be particularly cautious about buying gems from street traders, as there are some sophisticated scams operating that constantly trick would-be buyers.

Masks

Sri Lanka's rich history includes several folk traditions, many of which involve propitiation rites for various spirits and demons believed to have an influence on the lives of the locals. For such ceremonies, masks are carved that represent an amazing plethora of human, animal, divine, demonic and mythological characters. With their bright colours and striking expressions, these masks immediately attract the attention of foreign visitors, and, to meet demand, many masks are now made purely for the tourist market. The centre for mask carving is at Ambalangoda (*see pp78–9*) in the southwest, where there are museums explaining the legends behind the masks, workshops with carvers in action and showrooms displaying a huge choice of completed masks.

Other handicrafts

Wood is by no means the only medium of Sri Lankan craftspeople. Visitors to craft outlets are likely to be pleasantly surprised by the ingenuity of the artists in turning something as simple as a coconut shell into a smart item of home décor or a cute carving. Silverware and brassware have a distinctive Sri Lankan look, and something like an elaborate brass door-knocker makes an unusual souvenir, even if its function has been somewhat outdated by buzzers and bells. Lacquerware is a handicraft that seems purposely designed for travellers, being extremely light to carry, sturdy and generally functional too. Common items are bowls and trays. Leatherwork is also of high quality, and with comparatively cheap prices, this is a good place to pick up a new bag or pair

Ambalangoda is famous for its mask-carving tradition

of shoes. An odd reflection of the country's distant Dutch heritage is the lacework that can still be found along the south coast in towns like Galle and Weligama (*see pp80 and 88*), usually sold in the form of doilies and tablecloths. Finally, the colourful batiks on sale all over the island make striking wall-hangings or eye-catching shirts and sarongs.

Tea and spices

Most visitors include a visit to a tea plantation (*see pp108–9*) as part of their itinerary in Sri Lanka. After watching the tea pickers at work and the drying, grinding and fermenting of the tea, visitors are usually invited to buy a pack of their favourite blend, which makes a very practical souvenir or gift. Spice gardens are also interesting places to see cloves, black pepper or cinnamon growing on the plant. A pack of spices also makes a wonderful reminder of Sri Lanka's natural bounty, and, like tea, spices are light to carry, but bear in mind that there is a duty-free limit of 3kg (6.6lb) on tea.

WHERE TO BUY
Ambalangoda
Ariyapala Mask Museum
Fantastic array of bright masks.
426 Main Street. Tel: (091) 225 8373.
www.masksariyapalasl.com
Mask and Puppet Museum
Another stunning display of Sri Lankan masks and puppets.
428 Main Street.

Sri Lankan teas make distinctive gifts

MH Mettananda
A reputable mask carver in the heartland of this trade.
458 Main Street.

Colombo
Barefoot
Tasteful textiles made into stylish clothing and items of home décor.
704 Galle Road, Kollupitiya. Tel: 258 0114.
Craft Lanka
Textiles and a wide range of handicrafts.
101 Inner Flower Road. Tel: 257 3003.
House of Fashions
Ready-made garments at competitive prices in an air-conditioned complex.
28 Duplication Road, Colombo 4.
Tel: 250 4639.
Lakmedura
Small but attractive range of handmade textiles, crafts and objets d'art.
113 Dharmapala Mawatha, Colombo 7.
Tel: 233 5380.
Lakpahana
All kinds of handicrafts as well as lacework, batik and jewellery.
21 Rajakeeya Mawatha, Cinnamon Gardens. Tel: 269 8211.

Laksala

Fixed but fair prices on a wide range of Sri Lankan handicrafts.

60 York Street, Fort. Tel: 232 9247

Lanka Hands

Jewellery, crafts, toys, brassware, basketry and more at reasonable prices.

135 Bauddhaloka Mawatha, Bambalapitiya. Tel: 451 2311.

Mlesna Tea Centre

There are several outlets of this company specialising in tea.

Colombo Hilton, Majestic City, Liberty Plaza and the international airport.

Odel Unlimited

Huge range of clothing, books, tea and more, in a modern complex.

5 Alexandra Place, Cinnamon Gardens. Tel: 471 0200.

Paradise Road

Sculpture, ceramics, antique furniture, books, maps and other collectibles.

213 Dharmapala Road, Cinnamon Gardens. Tel: 268 6043.

Serendib

Paintings, sculpture, antiques, porcelain and prints are among the collectibles here.

361/1 Rosmead Place, Cinnamon Gardens. Tel: 567 4578.

Sri Lanka Gem & Jewellery Exchange

Two floors of shops selling gems and jewellery, and a testing laboratory.

Level 4 & 5, World Trade Centre, Bank of Ceylon Mawatha.

Galle

Olanda

Reproduction Dutch furniture, ceramic door knobs and religious statues.

30 Leyn Baan Street. Tel: 223 4398.

Cargills Department Store, Colombo

Textiles for sale in Kandy

South Ceylon Industrial Agency & Handicraft Factories (SCIA)

Watch items of lace, batik, leather and jewellery being crafted.
73A Kandewatta Road.
Tel: (091) 223 4304.

Hikkaduwa
Batik Studio
Wide range of eye-catching batiks.
Waulagoda Road.

Kandy
Daswanis
24-hour tailoring service with reasonable prices.
Queen's Hotel Building, Trincomalee Street. Tel: 222 3998.

Kandyan Art Association & Cultural Centre

Watch craftspeople at work and buy an item of brass or lacquerware.
Beside Kandy Lake.
Kandy Market
Fabrics, leather, shoes, batiks and handicrafts galore to be bargained for.
Station Road.

Matale
Matale Heritage Centre
Some lovely embroidery, batiks, brassware and carvings on display.
Sir Richard Aluvihara Mawatha.
Tel: 222 2404.

Entertainment

While there are plenty of sights and activities to keep visitors happy during the day in Sri Lanka, the country is not renowned for its nightlife. In fact, little happens at night outside Colombo, where most nightclubs are located in the top hotels. Performances of traditional music and dance are often put on especially for tourists, but are still worth watching for a taste of Sinhalese culture, especially the spectacularly acrobatic Kandyan dancers.

Towns along the south coast like Hikkaduwa cater for visitors who like to enjoy a drink and listen to music at night, and cinemas in Colombo show English-soundtracked films. If you happen to be in the country while an international cricket match is taking place, go along to witness the national mania for the sport.

Traditional music and dance

Cultural shows are occasionally staged at the Lionel Wendt Gallery & Theatre in Colombo, and there are daily performances by Kandyan dancers in various locations in Kandy. Watching the athletic movements of these supremely-fit dancers is one of the highlights of a visit to the country, and should not be missed. After thrilling the audience with their dancing and energetic drumming, the performers complete the show by walking across red-hot coals. If you want to photograph the performance, conditions are better at the Kandyan Art Association than at the Kandy Lake Club.

Kandy Lake Club
Sangamitta Mawatha, Kandy.

**Kandyan Art Association
& Cultural Centre**
Northern side of Kandy Lake, Kandy.

Lionel Wendt Gallery & Theatre
18 Guildford Crescent, Cinnamon Gardens, Colombo. Tel: 269 5794.

Theatre, classical music and exhibitions

Occasional performances of both Western and Sri Lankan dramas are held at the Lionel Wendt Gallery & Theatre (*see p51*), which also hosts frequent art exhibitions) and at the Elphinstone Theatre in Colombo. Cultural centres such as the British Council and Alliance Française feature art exhibitions and classical music performances from time to time. Check out local newspapers.

Alliance Française
11 Barnes Place, Cinnamon Gardens, Colombo. Tel: 269 4162.

British Council
49 Alfred House Gardens, Kollupitiya,
Colombo. Tel: 452 1521.

Elphinstone Theatre
Maradana Road, Maradana, Colombo.
Tel: 243 3635.

Lionel Wendt Gallery & Theatre
18 Guildford Crescent, Cinnamon
Gardens, Colombo. Tel: 269 5794.

Nightclubs, discos and karaoke

There is no shortage of places to go out
dancing in Colombo, but there are few
venues in the rest of the country. Also,
as most nightclubs and discos are
located in the fancy hotels, drink prices
are comparatively steep. If you feel like
bursting into song, check out one of the
well-equipped karaoke lounges.

Blue Elephant
Hilton Colombo, Lotus Road,
Colombo. Tel: 254 4644.

H₂O
447 Union Place, Cinnamon Gardens,
Colombo. Tel: 537 4444.

'Lava' Karaoke
Hilton Colombo, Lotus Road,
Colombo. Tel: 254 4644.

Legends
Majestic City, Galle Road, Colombo.

Sequel
Cinnamon Grand Hotel, Galle Road,
Colombo. Tel: 243 7437.

Showboat Karaoke
104 Reid Avenue, Colombo. Tel: 259 6958.

Bars and pubs

Bars and pubs as Westerners know them
are not a regular part of Sri Lankan life,
so those that do exist are catering for
the tourist trade. All of the top hotels
have a bar, many of them with beautiful
décor and romantic views, but be
prepared for high prices. Fortunately
there are plenty of alternatives in
Colombo, Kandy and on the coast
where you can soak up the local
atmosphere. For a taste of live music,
check out the Saxophone Jazz Club or
the Rhythm & Blues Bar in Colombo.

Andre and Sophia's Pub
29A Anagarika Dhamapala Mawatha,
Kandy.

Bradman Bar
Cricket Club Café, 34 Queens Road,
Colombo. Tel: 250 1384.

Chill Space Surf Café
Galle Road, Hikkaduwa.

Clancy's Irish Pub
29 Maitland Crescent, Cinnamon
Gardens, Colombo. Tel: 268 2945.

Galle Fort Hotel Bar
28 Church Street, Fort, Galle.
Tel: 223 2870.

Molly's Irish Pub & Restaurant
46/38 Nawam Mawatha, Slave Island,
Colombo. Tel: 254 3966.

The Pub
Dalada Vidiya, Kandy. Tel: 223 4868.

Pub Royale
Dalada Vidiya, Kandy.
Tel: 223 3026.

Rhythm & Blues Bar
19/1 Daisy Villa Avenue, Bambalapitiya,
Colombo.

Saxophone Jazz Club
46B Galle Road, Colombo. Tel: 233 4700.

Casinos

There are over 20 casinos in Colombo where you can find a game of roulette, blackjack or baccarat. Many of them are open 24 hours a day, and all try to outdo each other by offering punters free transportation there and free drinks and snacks. Some even offer a buffet dinner and live music. You will find that a few of them can be quite seedy, but the following are a few of the better establishments.

Pooja dancer, Kandy

Bally's Club
14 Dharmapala Mawatha, Colombo 3.
Tel: 257 3497.
Bellagio
430 R A De Mel Mawatha, Colombo 3.
Tel: 257 5271.
MGM Grand Casino
170 Galle Road, Colombo 4.
Tel: 259 1319.

Cinemas

As in many countries, cinemas in Sri Lanka have been adversely affected by the advent of VCRs and DVDs, and there are now no more than a handful of places in Colombo where you can watch a film on the big screen. As might be expected, they are generally located in or near shopping malls. If you are a lover of art-house films, check out the schedule at the British Council or Alliance Française.

Alliance Française
11 Barnes Place, Cinnamon Gardens, Colombo. Tel: 269 4162.
www.alliancefr.lk
British Council
49 Alfred House Gardens, Kollupitiya.
Tel: 452 1521.
www.britishcouncil.org/srilanka
Liberty Cinema
Opposite Liberty Plaza, Colombo.
Tel: 232 5264.
Majestic Cinema
Level 4, Majestic City, Bambalapitiya.
Tel: 258 1759.
Savoy Cinema
Galle Road, Wellawatta.

Children

Sri Lankans love children, so if you are travelling with one or more of them in tow, you are bound to be warmly welcomed at your hotel or guesthouse, as well as in restaurants. Travelling with children also guarantees more interaction with locals through their natural curiosity. However, whether your children actually enjoy themselves in Sri Lanka will depend on how adaptable they are.

There are no theme parks and few computer game arcades, but plenty of opportunities for fun both on the beach and in the hill country. Even the Ancient Cities can be enjoyable for the young if approached in an adventurous way. Safaris, cycle rides and snorkelling are just some of the activities available. If you can time

Children dressed up as nobility in a festival parade

your visit to coincide with one of the country's major festivals, such as the Kandy Perahera (*see p29*), your children will be delighted.

Animal watching

There is no shortage of guides offering safaris through national parks and wildlife sanctuaries, providing the chance to watch animals like elephants and leopards in their natural environment. Such tours do not come cheap, and there is no guarantee that you will see anything, but if you are lucky enough to make a few sightings, it will be an experience for all the family to remember.

There is only one zoo in Sri Lanka, located at Dehiwala, about 10km (6 miles) south of Colombo (*see p55*). It has a wide range of animals, including lots of birds and an aquarium. There is an elephant show each afternoon, but probably the best place to watch these gentle giants is at the Pinnawela Elephant Orphanage (*see pp74–5*), where many of them are youngsters. You can watch them playing in the river and even feed the babies with a milk bottle. If you want a ride on an elephant, head for the River Side Elephant Park, a few kilometres southwest of Kandy.

Beach games

Children are in their element on the beach and often need little supervision as they play on the sand and splash in the waves. In places like Hikkaduwa (*see p79*), where tourism is rapidly recovering from the effects of the tsunami, you can rent snorkelling equipment or take a ride in a glass-bottomed boat around coral reefs. Also interesting for children are turtle hatcheries (*see p77*), of which there are several along the south coast, where they can watch the tiny newborn creatures flapping their way across the beach to the sea, or even give them a helping hand.

Cycling tours

While children are not as enthralled as adults by the centuries-old sites of the Ancient Cities, exploring them can be turned into fun by organising a bicycle ride around the sites. In fact, cycling is the best way to get around the scattered sites of Polonnaruwa (*see pp122–4*) and Anuradhapura (*see pp127–9*) and bicycles are easy to rent locally, but make sure you take a long break in the middle of the day to avoid the fiercest heat.

Shows and festivals

Just like adults, children love to watch an exciting show or colourful festival parade. One performance that captivates everybody is that of the Kandyan drummers and dancers. If your visit coincides with a major festival, take your children along to join in the fun.

A herd of elephants at the orphanage in Pinnawela

Sport and leisure

Few people go to Sri Lanka for the sporting opportunitie
alone, yet a surprising amount are available on the island
The most popular sports among the locals are cricket and
rugby, and while you might not plan to play a team spor
like this during a short stay, it can be fun to go along and
watch a game, then improvise a game with others on the
beach. Also on the beach, water sports of all kinds are or
offer, including surfing, diving and deep-sea fishing.

There are a few golf courses in glorious locations and tennis courts in top-class hotels. Cycling is a good way to get around the Ancient Cities, and there are challenging routes for mountain-bike riders in the Hill Country. Hiking is yet another possibility, either to the summit of Adam's Peak (*see pp114–15*) or on gentler terrain in the hills around Kandy (*see pp60–65*) and Nuwara Eliya (*see pp105–7*).

Cricket

You don't have to travel far in Sri Lanka to realise that the whole country is cricket crazy. Groups of youngsters improvise a game on any patch of land available, often with nothing more than a stick for a bat and a rolled-up sock for a ball. When an international test match takes place, the whole country grinds to a halt for five days as the population remains glued to the commentary on TV and radio. Whether you know a googly from a yorker, or first slip from silly mid-on, it's well worth going along to watch a game.

The main international stadium is the **Premadasa Stadium** in Kettarama, and another popular venue is the **Sinhalese Sports Club** (SSC) in Cinnamon Gardens, Colombo (*see pp50–51*). There are also cricket stadiums in Galle, Kandy, Dambulla and Moratuwa. To obtain tickets for a match, contact the Board of Control for Cricket in Sri Lanka at *35 Maitland Place, Colombo (Tel: 268 1601).*

Cycling

Given the small size of Sri Lanka and the compact nature of its attractions, cycling around the countryside makes good sense. It is also an ideal way to have encounters with the local people. Bicycles for rent are easily found in tourist areas, and this is the best way to see the monuments of the Ancient Cities, especially at Anuradhapura (*see pp127–9*) and Polonnaruwa (*see pp122–4*).

For a more exciting ride through the rubber or tea estates in the hill country contact Adventure Sports Lanka (*see p161 for address*).

Golf and tennis

Green fees and club rental in Sri Lanka are much cheaper than in Western countries, and the beautifully landscaped courses are a joy to walk around. Best of the bunch is the **Victoria Golf Club** at Rajawella near Kandy (*Tel: (081) 237 6376*), but there are also very attractive courses at the **Nuwara Eliya Golf Club** (*Tel: (052) 222 2835*), which is at over 548m (1,798ft), and the **Royal Colombo Golf Club** (*Tel: 269 5431*) in Colombo. Also in Colombo, there are tennis courts at the **Colombo Hilton** (*Tel: 254 4644*), the **Cinnamon Grand** (*Tel: 243 7437*) and the **Sri Lanka Tennis Association** (*Tel: 533 7161*).

Hiking

The rugged hills that cover much of Sri Lanka make it ideal trekking country, although as yet there are no trekking agencies that organise tours. The most popular hike in the country is to the top of Adam's Peak (*see pp114–15*), a form of pilgrimage for Sri Lankans, who go to see what they believe to be a footprint of Buddha on the 2,243m (7,359ft) peak. Make the 7km (4$\frac{1}{2}$-mile) trek at night to enjoy the fabulous view at dawn. The best season for this hike is between December and May, although it can get crowded in January and February. The regions around Kandy (*see pp60–65*) and Nuwara Eliya (*see pp105–10*) are also excellent for exploring on foot.

A fairway on Nuwara Eliya Golf Course

Canoes on Beruwela beach, south of Colombo

Water sports

Apart from exploring the Ancient Cities, spending time on the beach is a top priority for visitors to Sri Lanka, so there are plenty of water sports to choose from. There are several scuba-diving operations around the country, which organise both dives for experienced divers and instruction for beginners. The best dive sites are along the west and south coasts, although there are others on the east coast. Because the movements of the monsoons affect these coasts differently, the diving season on the east coast is from May to September and on the west coast from November to April. Choose from open water dives, wreck dives or night dives. Some of the most reliable dive tour operators are **Scuba Safaris** (*Coral Gardens Hotel, Hikkaduwa. Tel: (091) 227 7023*), the **International Diving School** (*330 Galle Road, Hikkaduwa. Tel: (091) 438 3225*)

and **Underwater Safaris** (*25C Barnes Place, Cinnamon Gardens, Colombo. Tel: 269 4012*).

There is good snorkelling at Hikkaduwa (*see p79*) and Unawatuna (*see p88*) on the west and south coasts, where brilliant-coloured fish flit in and out of the various types of coral. On the east coast, one of the best spots for snorkelling is **Pigeon Island**, situated off the coast from Nilaveli Beach, just north of Trincomalee. At each of these locations, masks and flippers are available to rent. Unfortunately, many areas of coral have degenerated due to visitors breaking off pretty pieces as souvenirs. If you find yourself tempted to do the same (despite the dubious legality of doing so), just remind yourself that it will never look as good in your bathroom a it does under the sea. Besides, many types of coral can cause painful blistering if they come into contact with the skin.

Surfing is also very popular, and surfboards and wet suits are easy to hire in the most popular places. There are good surfing beaches on the south and west coasts, particularly at Hikkaduwa and Mirissa (*see p88*), where the best waves come from November to April. However, many think that the best surfing beach in the country is at Arugam Bay (*see p130*), currently closed due to the security situation in this region.

Windsurfing is possible, but only on the west coast of the island around Bentota (*see pp77–8*), where places like **Club Inter Sport** (*Bentota Beach Hotel, Bentota. Tel: (034) 227 5178*) rent out windsurfing equipment, and also offer deep-sea fishing tours.

Swimming of course needs no special equipment and there are some glorious beaches on the west, south and east coasts where conditions are ideal. However, the shifting monsoons can cause deadly riptides, so keep an eye open for warning signs. Most good hotels have swimming pools, which can be a more relaxing alternative, especially if you are travelling with children.

Not all water sports are found on the beach. The rugged hill country provides ideal conditions for white-water rafting, an experience guaranteed to get your heart pumping. Companies like **Adventure Sports Lanka** (*366/3 Rendapola Horagahakanda Lane, Talangama, Koswatta. Tel: (011) 279 1584. www.actionlanka.com*) can arrange for you to take on the grade-4 rapids on the Kelani River (*see pp58–9*), southwest of Kandy. Some tours include canoeing on rivers and reservoirs.

Surfing near Pottuvil Point on the east coast, currently off-limits to tourists

Food and drink

For many visitors to Sri Lanka, eating is a mixture o[f] delight and frustration. Delight comes from discovering [a] delicious curry sauce or a tasty tropical fruit, whil[e] frustration comes from over-spicy dishes, poorly prepare[d] Western food or an interminable wait for the food t[o] appear. However, this is changing fast, and a rash o[f] independent restaurants has sprung up recently, offerin[g] good-quality Western food and local dishes that ar[e] palatable to outsiders. Not to be overlooked are street stall[s] which often sell tasty snacks for next to nothing.

WHAT TO EAT AND DRINK
Rice and curry

Sri Lankans' staple food is rice and curry, frequently eaten with a bowl of *dahl* (lentil soup) and fried vegetables. Although this may sound boring, there is a huge variety of types of curry sauce – thick or thin, mild or fiery – so there is plenty of room to explore. The herbs and spices used in the curry sauces include caraway and cardamom, cloves and garlic, mustard seeds and chilli, and each cook has his or her own special combination. Sri Lankans like their food very spicy, so be cautious with your first taste if eating in a local restaurant or café. If it does set your mouth on fire, cool it down with yoghurt and cucumber. Unfortunately, much of the rice served in these local food shops is of poor quality, making another unpredictable element to the meal. One solution is to eat in hotels and tourist restaurants, where the curries are milder but much more expensive.

Eating etiquette

Sri Lankans eat with their right hand, mixing a small ball of rice and curry with the thumb and fingertips, then lifting it on cupped fingers and sliding it into the mouth with the thumb. They swear that this is the only way to appreciate the full flavour of a good meal, but they do not expect foreigners to follow suit, so will usually rustle up a spoon and/or fork for visitors. Feel free to act like the locals, but it is a tricky technique to master, and you may end up with more curry on your clothes than in your mouth.

Hoppers and *rotis*

The Sri Lankan diet is not exclusively about rice and curry. The traditional breakfast consists of *hoppers*, a kind of pancake that is soft inside but crispy outside, often with an egg in the middle. Another variation is the *string hopper*, which is made of steamed noodles and is often eaten as an accompaniment to curry in place of rice. *Rotis*, also a kind of pancake, are sold from mobile stalls that can be found on street corners all over the country, and make a good filling snack with sweet or savoury fillings.

Short eats and lunch packets

These two options are great for a quick, cheap and tasty lunch. Short eats are snacks like meat and vegetable patties that are set out on tables. Just eat as many as you like and you will be charged accordingly. Lunch packets are sold on street corners and in markets throughout the country between around 11am and 2pm, and consist of a portion of rice, a vegetable and meat curry, and chilli sauce, all wrapped up in a neat package to take away.

Desserts and fruits

Most Sri Lankans have a sweet tooth and there are many unusual desserts available in the country. One of the most intriguing is *wattalappam*, a kind of caramel pudding with coconut. *Jaggery* is a sweetener made from the syrup of the kitul palm, and is used to make many desserts and sweets, such as *kalu dodol*, a delicious concoction of cashew nuts, coconut milk and *jaggery*. Some of the desserts may be just too sweet for Westerners, but this is more than made up for by the proliferation of tropical fruits. Mangoes, guavas, durians, jackfruits, mangosteens, rambutans, custard apples and papayas are all packed with juicy goodness.

Drinks

The vast range of fruits makes for great fruit juices and shakes. One of the best ways to quench thirst is *thambili*, the juice of the king coconut. Tap water is not safe to drink, so stick to mineral water.

Good coffee is rare, but Sri Lankan tea is world famous, and a good cup of Broken Orange Pekoe is a taste to savour. Although tea is served in most restaurants and cafés, it comes ready

A selection of seafood from the Indian Ocean

mixed with hot milk and sugar, which is not to everyone's taste.

Locally brewed beer is quite good, but comparatively expensive, while the local wine is rather sweet for most Western tastes. Californian wine is the only other wine readily available.

WHERE TO EAT

Eating out in Sri Lanka can be very cheap indeed. For example, a lunch packet or set meal in a local restaurant costs less than Rs100. Even in the top hotels, a blow-out meal will rarely set you back more than Rs1,500.

A ten per cent service charge is included in the price, and five-star hotels add another ten per cent, but this generally goes to the owner, not the staff, so it is thoughtful to leave a small tip if you are happy with the service.

Colombo Pettah fruit merchants

In the restaurant listings below, the following symbols have been used to indicate the average cost of a meal per person, not including alcohol.

★   under Rs800
★★   from Rs800–1400
★★★   over Rs1400

Colombo

Café 64 ★

Good for a quick bite or takeaway biriyani, *kottu* (filled pancake) or shawarma. Barbecue nights (booking recommended) take place on the terrace on Friday and Saturday night.
Galadari Hotel,
64 Lotus Road.
Tel: 254 4544,
ext 326. Open: daily
7am–11pm.

Verandah Restaurant ★

Typical English high tea at one of Asia's oldest hotels, dating back to 1874.
Galle Face Hotel,
2 Kollupitiya Road,
Colombo 3.
Tel: 254 1010.
Open: daily 10am–11pm.

Cricket Club Café ★★

Tasty snacks and sandwiches surrounded by cricket memorabilia in a fashionable district of Colombo.
34 Queens Road (off Duplication Road).
Tel: 250 1384. Open: daily 11am–11pm.

Deli Market ★★

A food centre with numerous kiosks serving an array of Sri Lankan and international dishes.
3rd floor, World Trade Centre, Echelon Square, Fort. Open: daily 9am–11pm.

Gallery Café ★★

Stylish ambience in leafy part of town attracts trendy types to feast on local, French and Italian cuisine. Best frozen margarita in Colombo.
Paradise Road,
2 Alfred House Road.
Tel: 258 2162. Open: daily 10am–10pm.

InsideOut ★★

Home-from-home ambience meets urban chic in this converted house, which has alfresco dining in the garden. Try lamb curry or delicious beef burgers grilled with pineapple. Free Wi-Fi access.
446 Pannipitiya Road, Pellawatta, Battaramulla.
Tel: 278 5120.
Open: Mon–Thur
10.30am–10pm; Fri–Sun 11am–11pm.

The Mango Tree ★★

Stylishly authentic north Indian restaurant serving great selection of vegetarian dishes and fresh tandoori bread.
82 Dharmapala Mw. Cinnamon Gardens.
Tel: 537 9790.
Open: daily noon–3pm, 7–10pm.

Palmyrah ★★

Classic Sri Lankan favourites; especially Jaffna cuisine, seafood crêpes and baked crab starters, served in a modern restaurant.
Hotel Renuka,
328 Galle Road.
Tel: 257 3598.
Open: daily noon–2.30pm & 7–11.30pm.

Sakura Japanese Restaurant ★★

Sushi and sashimi are just a few of the traditional meals served in this eatery popular with Japanese tourists.
14 Rheinland Place.
Tel: 257 3877.
Open: daily 11am–11pm.

Trainspotters ★★

Trendy restaurant with views of the sea and railway track, hence its name. A great selection of meat and vegetarian dishes.
Global Towers,
11 Station Avenue.
Tel: 259 1000.
Open: daily 24 hours.

The Bayleaf ★★★

A former colonial villa turned into a sophisticated restaurant serving international and local cuisine.
79 Gregory's Road,
Cinnamon Gardens.
Tel: 269 5920. Open: daily for lunch and dinner.

Curry Leaf ★★★

Delicious Sri Lankan dishes, with regional specialities, in a garden setting. Dinner only.
Colombo Hilton,
Lotus Road, Fort.
Tel: 254 4644. Open daily 7pm–12am.

Lavinia Breeze ★★★

It's well worth pushing the boat out in this romantic restaurant on the beach specialising in fusion cuisine.
43/7 Beach Road,
off De Saram Road,
Mount Lavinia.

Tel: 420 5183. Open: daily for lunch and dinner.

Saffron Restaurant ★★★

Unmissable for a different take on Sri Lankan and Indian food in plush surroundings.
Trans-Asia Hotel,
115 Sir Chitampalam A Gardiner Mawatha.
Tel: 249 1944.
Open: daily 12–2pm & 7–11pm.

Dehiwela

Café Asiana ★

Sumptuous Asian and international cuisine and close to the zoo.
97 Hill Street.
Tel: 420 2003.
cafe2asiana@yahoo.com.
Open: daily.

Galle

Pedlars Inn ★

Delightful café in former Dutch villa specialising in yummy chocolate brownies, right in the heart of Galle Fort.
92 Pedlar Street.
No telephone.
Open: daily 10am–6pm.

Rampart Hotel ★★

Tasty Sri Lankan and Western food served on a balcony overlooking the old town ramparts.

31 Rampart Street.
Tel: 438 0103.

Lady Hill ★★★

A spectacular rooftop restaurant with both set and à la carte menus.
The Lady Hill Hotel,
29 Upper Dickson Road.
Tel: (091) 224 4322.
www.ladyhillsl.com

Hikkaduwa

Cool Spot ★

Dinky little café that has been dishing out rice and noodles for three decades.
Galle Road, Wewala.
Open: daily 9am–10pm.

Refresh Café ★

Hugely popular for seafood, fresh fish, plus Italian and Chinese offerings.
384 Galle Road.
Tel: (091) 227 7810.
refresh@sri.lanka.net.
Open: till late.

Spaghetti & Co ★★

Italian pizza and pasta served in casual colonial-style garden villa.
Galle Road, Thiranagama Hikkaduwa.
Open: all day.

Firefly ★★★

Creative cuisine using seafood and local produce in a beautifully

The Cricket Club Café, Colombo

Curry and vegetables, Sri Lankan style

restored villa, making a welcome change from Hikkaduwa's cafés.
364 Galle Road,
Dodonaduwa.
Tel: (091) 545 1641.
Open: evenings only.

Kandy
Olde Empire ★
Classic colonial haunt turning out a decent curry, and lunch packets too.
Olde Empire Hotel,
21 Temple Street.
Tel: (081) 222 4284.
White House ★
Long-established local eatery renowned for its extensive range of noodles, curries, rice and pasta dishes.
Dalada Vidaya.
Tel: (081) 222 3393.
Open: all day.
The Pub ★★
Reasonable Western dishes like spaghetti, plus draught beer and imported wines.
36 Dalada Vidiya.
Tel: (081) 223 4868.

Matale
Matale Heritage
Centre ★★★
Excellent lunch stop if travelling to the

Ancient Cities. The centre showcases 25 Sri Lankan dishes and traditional handicrafts in a village atmosphere. Food is served on a ledge overlooking a jungle, but you need to give three days' notice for this unique feast.
The Wallauwa,
33 Sir Richard Aluvihare
Mawatha, Aluvihare,
Matale.
Tel: (066) 222 2404.
Open: Mon–Sat
9.30am–4.30pm.

Nuwara Eliya
Ambals ★
Popular vegetarian restaurant right in the heart of town.
New Bazaar Street.
Open: Mon–Sat.
The Grand Hotel
Cafeteria ★★
Relaxing cafeteria-style restaurant by the hotel gates, specialising in Indian cuisine.
Grand Hotel Road.
Tel: (052) 222 2881.
Open: daily.
Hill Club ★★★
Dress up for a memorable five-course set dinner served by waiters in white gloves.

Grand Hotel Road.
Tel: (052) 222 2881.

Tissamaharama
Refresh Café ★★
Delightful garden setting. Casual ambience and serving best blow-out curry in town.
Akurugoda.
Tel: (047) 223 7357.
Open: for lunch and dinner.

Vegetarian food
If you are vegetarian you are in for a treat as there are so many home-grown vegetables and fruits, and staples such as rice and noodles, in Sri Lanka. With 15 per cent of the population hailing from south India where vegetarian specialities are prominent, you'll find south Indian restaurants in Colombo. Throughout the island, you will find vegetarian dishes on many menus. The oil normally used for cooking is coconut oil, but if you are at all unsure, just ask. Hotels and guesthouses will gladly comply with any special requests.

A taste of Sri Lanka

Sri Lankan cuisine is rich and varied, combining indigenous Sinhalese and Tamil foundations with additional Malay, Portuguese, Dutch and British influences. The island enjoys an abundant supply of fresh seafood from the surrounding waters. The fertile lowlands provide a rich selection of tropical fruits, while the forested hills offer jungle delicacies such as venison and wild boar.

As in much of tropical Asia, rice is the staple food for Sri Lankans of all races. It is served with a selection of spicy curries together with chutney, pickles and sambals as garnishes. In Sri Lanka, the art of cooking has traditionally been a family affair, and many of the best recipes are passed on, mother to daughter, generation to generation, with never a cookbook in sight. In recent years, however, as the island's tourist industry has matured, master chefs at some of the country's top hotels have introduced traditional Sri Lankan cuisine to their menus. One such is Trevor Fernando, Executive Chef of Club Hotel Dolphin in Waikkal, near Negombo. The following dishes, taken from his extensive repertoire, represent three popular traditional curries – one chicken, one seafood and one pork. *Bon appetit* or, as they say in Sinhalese, *rasawath kama*!

Kukulmas Kariya
(Sri Lankan Chicken Curry)
Cut the chicken into pieces and let the water drain off. Heat some oil in a saucepan and lightly fry a mix of sliced garlic, ginger, green chillies, curry leaves and lemon grass. Then add chilli powder, curry powder,

A Sri Lankan chef preparing *hoppers*

pepper, turmeric, cardamom and cloves and continue to fry lightly. Add sliced tomatoes and onion and let the mixture cook for a while before adding chicken and coconut milk. Simmer until tender. Serve with boiled long-grain rice or *roti*. Garnish with papadum and a selection of chutneys.

Pokirissan (Lobster Curry)

Split the lobster into two, separate the flesh and cut it into small pieces. Wash the shell, boil and keep it aside. Heat some butter in a saucepan and fry sliced garlic, onion, green chillies, ginger and curry leaves to a golden brown colour. Add chilli powder, turmeric powder and curry powder and fry lightly for some time. Add the lobster pieces. After a few minutes add salt, cardamom, cloves and flour with coconut milk. Simmer over a moderate heat. Flavour with lime juice and stuff into the lobster shells. Serve with coconut *roti* or long-grain saffron rice.

Wal Uru Mus (Curried Wild Boar)

Cut the wild boar meat into small, bite-sized pieces, wash thoroughly, place in a saucepan and fry gently with a mix of dried chilli powder, green chillies, black pepper, curry powder, salt, garlic, cardamom and red onions. Mix well, add two to three cups of water, and cook slowly over a moderate heat until done.

An array of the finest Sri Lankan cuisine

Accompaniments

Sri Lankan cuisine is characterised by a wide range and variety of side dishes. These traditionally include *mallum*, a preparation in which a fruit, edible root, leaf or vegetable is finely shredded or grated and cooked with coconut; *moju*, a type of preserved fish or meat preparation, usually acidic, served like pickle or chutney; and *sambal*, a blend of vegetable, coconut or other fruits with seasoning – usually onions and chillies – added.

Hotels and accommodation

Sri Lanka is not a large or highly developed island, but its reputation as a paradise isle for tourists ensures a wide range of accommodation throughout the country. You can find everything from five-star luxury hotels with all the facilities you might need down to a rented room in a family house. It has to be said, however, that good options for budget travellers are few and far between, and dormitories with several beds are almost nonexistent.

The official star-rating system for hotels is generally reliable, but can be erratic at the lower end. Most rooms include a private bathroom, mosquito meshing on the windows and doors, plus a fan or air conditioning. Several hotels have rooms at various prices, reflecting the facilities available or aspects such as size of room and view, so it's worth checking out a few before you decide.

Prices and booking

As a rule, top hotels in Sri Lanka quote their prices in US dollars, while small guesthouses give their rates in rupees. As with most destinations, price reflects quality, and rates vary from a few dollars for a small, windowless room to hundreds of dollars for a penthouse suite with a glorious view. Prices also vary drastically according to the season, which in itself varies in different parts of the island. High season on the western and southern coasts is from mid-December to March, on the eastern coast from April to September, in Kandy and the Ancient Cities from July to August, and in Nuwara Eliya from March to May. During these periods, it is advisable to have a prior booking, which is easily done by visiting *www.srilanka.com*. Prices in the listings below are for the high season. If you are travelling during the low season, you may be able to negotiate up to 50 per cent discount, depending on your bargaining ability.

Guesthouses

If you dislike staying in large, impersonal places, then consider one of the country's many guesthouses. The owners will usually go out of their way to make you feel at home and can also help you get around to see the sights. Some guesthouses are little more than basic shacks, while at the top end there are some luxurious colonial mansions that would be ideal for honeymooners.

Hotels

Sri Lanka's top hotels tend to be either very modern and very large, with all kinds of facilities such as business centres, gyms and tennis courts, or former colonial mansions that are full of character and offer more personalised service but fewer facilities. Most of these top-end places tend to be concentrated in Colombo and along the western and southern coasts. Mid-range hotels vary a lot in what they offer, so it's best to look first if you can. There is no clear distinction in Sri Lanka between hotels, guesthouses, lodges and inns, and some of the well-run guesthouses are better than cheap hotels.

National park bungalows

If you plan to spend some time observing wildlife in one of the main national parks (Horton Plains, Uda Walawe, Gal Oya and Wasgomuwa), it is possible to stay in a bungalow run by the **Department of Wildlife Conservation** (*382 New Kandy Road, Malambe. Tel: 256 0380. Fax: 274 4301. www.dwlc.lk*). Costs are in the region of £20 per night per person, plus a 'service charge' of another £20 per person per stay.

Rest houses

There are rest houses scattered around the island that were originally built by the Dutch to house travelling officials, and were then taken over by the British for a similar purpose. Many are now run by the Ceylon Hotels Corporation and can provide an idyllic place to rest up, particularly since they were built to take advantage of the best views in the area. Some are rather run-down but others are maintained with pride and are a pleasure to stay in.

The Galle Face Hotel in Colombo

WHERE TO STAY

In the accommodation listings below, the following symbols have been used to indicate the cost of a double room in high season.

★   under Rs8,000
★★ from Rs8,000–13,000
★★★ over Rs13,000

Ahungalla
Heritance
Ahungalla ★★★
Refurbished since the tsunami, this impressive hotel has access to beach, eight restaurants and bars, shopping arcade and library.
Tel: (091) 555 5000;
fax: (091) 555 5055;
ahungalla@
heritancehotels.com;
www.heritancehotels.com

Anuradhapura
Nuwarawewa
Resthouse ★
Lakeside setting, small pool and restaurant with local and western food.
New Town.
Tel: (025) 222 1414;
hotels@quickshaws.com;
www.quickshaws.com
Tissawewa Grand ★★
Stylish décor in air-conditioned rooms

plus cottage room for families. No alcohol is served.
Sacred City.
Tel: (025) 222 2299;
hotels@quickshaws.com;
www.quickshaws.com

Bentota
Induruwa Beach
Resort ★
Large, all-inclusive hotel with 90 rooms and two pools overlooking gorgeous beach.
Tel: (011) 257 5382;
fax: (011) 257 5038;
villaocn@sltnet.lk;
www.villaoceanhotels.com
Bentota Beach Hotel ★★
Reminiscent of a 17th-century Dutch fort with 133 a/c stylish rooms, several restaurants and bars and swimming pool. Ayurvedic centre and boat and elephant rides on the beach.
Tel: (034) 227 5176;
fax: (034) 227 5179;
bbh@keels.com;
www.johnkeellshotels.com
Serendib Hotel ★★
All-inclusive option for families in the ambience of an 18th-century Dutch seaside village. 90 rooms, spa, lap pool and water sports.

Tel: (034) 227 5248;
fax: (034) 227 5353;
inquiries@
serendibleisure.lk;
www.serendibleisure.com

Beruwala
Riverina Hotel ★★
Popular with package tourists, with five restaurants and bars, discotheque, ayurvedic treatments and water sports.
Kaluwamodera.
Tel: (034) 227 6044;
fax: (034) 227 6047;
riverina@confifi.net;
www.riverinahotel.com

Colombo
Mrs Padmini
Nanayakkara's ★
Cosy rooms in one of Colombo's better districts, with breakfast included.
20 Chelsea Gardens,
Kollupitiya.
Tel: 227 8758.
Havelock Place
Bungalow ★★
Intimate upmarket six-roomed boutique hotel with stone courtyards, Jacuzzi and pool.
6 Havelock Place.
Tel: 258 5191; manager@
havelockbungalow.com;
www.havelockbungalow.com

Ranjit's Ambalama ★★
Small but friendly
guesthouse with
leafy courtyard.
53/19 Torrington Avenue,
Cinnamon Gardens.
Tel: 268 5067.

Sapphire ★★
This small hotel has
40 rooms, all with
air conditioning, TV,
phone and fridge.
371 Galle Road,
Wellawatta. Tel: 236 3306;
www.manaali.com/hotel
sapphire.htm

Cinnamon Grand Hotel
(formerly Oberoi) ★★★
Totally refurbished and
rebranded, this swish
hotel is centrally located.
Eleven restaurants
and bars, spa, swimming
pool.
77 Galle Road.
Tel: 243 7437;
fax: 244 9280; info@
cinnamonhotels.com;
www.cinnamonhotels.com

Galadari Hotel ★★★
Five-star hotel with good
restaurants, lively bars
and great view of the sea.
64 Lotus Road, Fort.
Tel: 254 4544;
fax: 254 9875;
info@galadarihotel.lk;
www.galadarihotel.com

Galle Face Hotel ★★★
A mid-19th-century
building that exudes
great charm (*see p43*).
2 Kollupitiya Road,
Kollupitiya. Tel: 254 1010;
fax: 254 1072;
reservations@
gallefacehotel.net;
www.gallefacehotel.com

Hilton ★★★
Value for money and
with a choice of ten
restaurants and bars.
2 Sir Chittampalam A
Gardiner Mawatha.
Tel: 249 2492;
fax: 254 4657;
colombo@hilton.com;
www.hilton.com

Mount Lavinia ★★★
Former governor's
residence with beautiful,
colonial-style rooms or
more contemporary sea-
and garden-facing rooms.
100 Hotel Road, Mount
Lavinia. Tel: 271 5221;
fax: 273 0726;
mount.lavinia@
mtlavinia.com; www.
mountlaviniahotel.com

Trans-Asia ★★★
Every conceivable
luxury and facility at
this huge hotel
overlooking Beira Lake.
Contemporary-styled
rooms (one for the
disabled), numerous bars
and restaurants and
friendly service.
115 Sir Chittampalam A
Gardiner Mawatha.
Tel: 249 1000;
fax: 244 9184; tah_asia@
transasiahotel.com;
www.transasiahotel.com

Dambulla
Heritance
Kandalama ★★★
Beautiful hotel built into
cliffside, endowed with
minimalist-style rooms
appealing to well-heeled
couples and families
seeking both culture
and relaxation.

The pool at the Trans-Asia Hotel, Colombo

Tel: (066) 555 5000;
fax: (066) 555 5055;
kandalama@
heritancehotels.com;
www.heritancehotels.com

Galle
Amangalla ★★★
Authentic colonial
400-year-old landmark
building located in the
historic fort.
10 Church Street.
Tel: (091) 223 3388;
fax: (091) 223 3355;
amangalla@
amanresorts.com;
www.amanresorts.com
Galle Fort Hotel ★★★
Imaginative and stylish
conversion from an
old Dutch warehouse
and better value than
other top hotels in Galle.

28 Church Street.
Tel: (091) 223 2870;
www.galleforthotel.com
The Lighthouse ★★★
Sri Lanka interior
design at its finest in
this 60-roomed
retreat.
Dadella.
Tel: (091) 222 3744;
fax: (091) 222 4021;
lighthouse@lighthouse.lk;
www.lighthouse.
jetwingsrilanka.com

Habarana
Chaaya Village ★★
Beautifully renovated
rustic chalet-style
complex of 108
rooms in spacious
gardens.
Tel: (066) 227 0047;
www.chaayahotels.com

Hikkaduwa
Coral Gardens ★★
A spacious beach-
front property, with
several restaurants,
two pools plus
entertainment and
water sports.
Galle Road.
Tel: (091) 227 7188;
fax: (091) 227 7189;
www.chaayahotels.com

Kalutara
Tangerine Beach Hotel ★★
Value-for-money
stylish beachside hotel
with garden full of
coconut palms, plus
pool, gym and health
centre.
Tel: (034) 223 7295;
fax: (034) 223 7794;
tangerinebeach@
tangerinehotels.com;
www.tangerinehotels.com

Kandy
Chaaya Citadel ★★
Lovely hillside setting
with 121 rooms,
pool and two
restaurants.
124 Srimath Kuda
Ratwatta Mawatha.
Tel: (081) 223 4365;
fax: (081) 223 3395;
www.chaayahotels.com

The Chaaya Citadel Hotel near Kandy

Mahaweli Reach Hotel ★★★
Calm and tranquillity in this sophisticated hotel on the Mahaweli River.
35 PBA Weerakoon Mawatha.
Tel: (081) 447 2727;
sales@mahaweli.com;
www.mahaweli.com

Negombo

Club Hotel Dolphin ★
This 152-roomed hotel offers all-inclusive options. Nightly entertainment, huge pool and water sports.
Kammala South, Waikkal.
Tel: (031) 227 7788;
fax: (031) 227 9437;
inquiries@ serendibleisure.lk;
www.serendibleisure.com

Goldi Sands Hotel ★
Beachfront hotel with 75 a/c rooms. Theme nights, cultural and fashion shows.
Ethukala.
Tel: (031) 227 9021;
fax: (031) 227 8019;
goldi@eureka.lk;
www.goldisands.com

Nuwara Eliya

Grand Hotel ★★
Stylish club atmosphere, billiard room, coffee shop, supper club and bar. Just around the corner from golf course.
Grand Hotel Road.
Tel: (052) 222 2881;
fax: (052) 222 2264;
grand@tangerinehotels. com;
www.tangerinehotels.com

St Andrews Hotel ★★
Olde England in Sri Lanka's hill country with four-poster beds.
10 St Andrews Drive.
Tel: (052) 222 3031;
fax: (052) 222 3153;
standrew@eureka.lk;
www.jetwing.com

The Tea Factory ★★
Cleverly converted tea factory with 57 loft rooms.
Kandapola.
Tel: (052) 222 9600;
fax: (052) 222 9606;
fom.teafactory@ aitkenspence.lk; www. aitkenspencehotels.net

Hill Club ★★★
Classic colonial haunt, with reading room.
Grand Hotel Road.
Tel: (052) 222 2653;
fax: (052) 222 2654;
www.hillclubsrilanka.net

Sigiriya

Sigiriya Hotel ★
Unpretentious hotel beneath Sigiriya Rock.
Tel: (066) 228 6821;
inquiries@ serendibleisure.com;
www.serendibleisure.com

Jetwing Vil Uyana ★★★
Rural luxury in this complex of 25 rustic chalets. Spa, gym and ayurvedic treatments.
Rangirigama.
Tel: (066) 492 3584;
fax: (066) 228 6005;
viluyana@wow.lk;
www.jetwing.com

Tissamaharama

Priyankara Hotel ★
Cheap and cheerful 26-roomed hotel.
Kataragama Road.
Tel: (047) 223 7206;
fax: (047) 223 7326;
priyankara@sltnet.lk;
www.priyankarahotel.com

Yala Village ★★
Rustic chalets in this eco-friendly resort.
Yala Safari Park.
Tel/fax: (047) 223 9450;
www.chaayahotels.com

Weligama

Bay Beach Hotel ★
Simple accommodation for budget travellers.
Kapparatota.
Tel/fax: (041) 225 0201;
baybeachhotel@sltnet.lk;
www.baybeachhotel.com

Practical guide

Arriving

Visas

Citizens from over 50 countries, including the UK, USA, Canada, Australia and New Zealand, are given a tourist visa on arrival valid for 30 days. If you plan a longer stay, consult the Sri Lankan Embassy in your own country, or check out the latest regulations at *www.immigration.gov.lk*. Visa extensions are possible for up to three months from the **Department of Immigration** (*41 Ananda Rajakaruna Mawatha, Colombo 10. Tel: 532 9000. Open: Mon–Fri 9am–4.30pm*).

By air

All visitors (apart from those on cruise ships; *see right*) arrive at Bandaranaike International Airport, also referred to as Katunayake Airport after the district in which it is located, about 35km (22 miles) north of Colombo. Scheduled airlines flying to Sri Lanka include Air Arabia, Cathay Pacific, Emirates, Etihad Airways, Indian Airlines, Jet Airways, Kuwait Airways, Malaysian Airlines, Qatar Airways, Royal Jordanian, Saudi Air, Singapore Airlines, Sri Lankan Airlines and Thai Airways.

At the airport is a 24-hour currency exchange office and a hotel reservation desk run by the Ceylon Tourist Board. Airport tax is now included in the cost of your airline ticket.

Buses 240 and 187 run from the airport to the centre of Colombo, but you may find it more convenient to take a taxi. This costs around 1,500 rupees and the journey takes a good 1 1/2 hours. For information about arrivals and departures, phone the airport's hotline at *019 733 2424* or *019 733 1377*.

By sea

The only people who arrive by sea in Sri Lanka are those on cruises during the season (Oct–May). They may stop off for a day or so in Colombo as part of a cruise that takes in other idyllic islands. For cruise information, check out *www.cruisecompete.com*

Camping

There are no official campsites in Sri Lanka except at Bundala Bird Sanctuary and Uda Walawe National Park (*see p146*). Tour companies that arrange adventure treks will provide any equipment necessary.

Children

There are no particular problems in travelling with children in Sri Lanka; in fact, their presence is likely to bring interesting encounters with locals. Baby foods and other items like nappies are available in the big supermarkets in Colombo.

Climate

Sri Lanka has a tropical climate, and most of the island has an average annual temperature of 30°C (86°F), although in the highlands around Nuwara Eliya it can drop below 10°C (50°F) at night from December to March. The southwesterly monsoon brings rain to the west and south coasts from May to September, while the northeasterly monsoon wets the east and north coasts from October to January. The driest time in Kandy in the hill country is from January until April. However, just to complicate things, the weather does not always follow expected patterns, so do not be surprised to see rain at any time. Carrying an umbrella is a wise move, both to keep you dry and to fend off the fierce heat of the midday sun.

Crime

Sri Lanka is no better or worse than other countries in terms of petty crimes like pickpocketing and bag snatching. Remember that foreigners are likely targets as they are seen to be rich, so be particularly careful with your

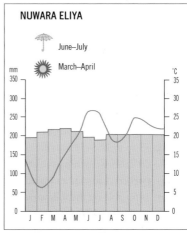

NUWARA ELIYA

June–July

March–April

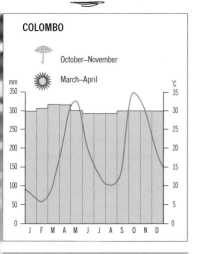

COLOMBO

October–November

March–April

WEATHER CONVERSION CHART

25.4mm = 1 inch

$°F = 1.8 \times °C + 32$

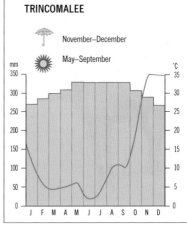

TRINCOMALEE

November–December

May–September

possessions in crowded places like shopping centres or buses. Also keep your hotel door locked and windows closed when out, as not only thieves but also monkeys might slip in.

The main trouble for tourists comes from those 'guides' who befriend you at the airport or on the street, offering to find you a good hotel, show you good places to eat and arrange an economical purchase of gems. Commissions are given by almost every tourist-related business, and there are plenty of touts trying to get their share. A polite but firm refusal is usually an effective way of dealing with such offers.

Customs regulations

For visits up to 90 days, you can bring in baggage up to US$125 duty free and you should declare anything valuable, such as jewellery, cameras and watches. No duty is payable on the following: 2 bottles of wine, 1.5 litres of spirits,

0.25 litres of toilet water, a small quantity of perfume and gifts up to US$250. On arrival you can buy duty free goods at the Sri Lanka Duty Free shop up to the value of US$187.50, provided no other goods are brought from abroad. Any excess is dutiable at the normal rates. For further details visit *www.customs.gov.lk*

Driving

While it is possible to rent a self-drive car in Sri Lanka, very few people do. The simple reason is that for a little extra you can hire a driver too and not have to worry about finding the right route or dealing with the unpredictable traffic. If you do decide to go it alone, according to the Sri Lankan Highway Code you should drive on the left at speeds no greater than 56kph (35mph) in urban areas and no more than 72kph (45mph) in rural areas. Watch out for potholes that can destroy a tyre or even a wheel in an instant.

Plenty of taxi drivers are happy to work on a daily basis for around Rs3,300 (£20) a day, including all costs such as petrol, meals and accommodation, but it's best to talk things over in detail first. Remember that the driver will probably also get a commission from most attractions and restaurants that you visit. For self-drive hire or car with driver, contact one of the following companies.

Quickshaws Tours
3 Kalinga Place, Havelock Town, Colombo. Tel: 258 3133.
www.quickshaws.com

Mounted policeman in Kandy

Walkers Tours

130 Glennie Sreet, Colombo 2.
Tel: 230 6719. www.walkerstours.com

Electricity

The electricity supply in Sri Lanka is 230V, 50 cycles AC. Most sockets take plugs with three round pins, and adaptors are sold in electrical stores. Electricity cuts and fluctuating current are common, so if you are travelling with a laptop computer, it's a good idea to get a voltage stabiliser from an electrical supply store.

Embassies and consulates

All embassies and consulates in Sri Lanka are located in Colombo.

Australia

21 Gregory's Road, Cinnamon Gardens, Colombo 7. Tel: 246 3200.
www.srilanka.embassy.gov.au

Canada

5 Gregory's Road, Cinnamon Gardens, Colombo 7. Tel: (011) 522 6232.
clmbo@international.gc.ca.
www.dfait-maeci.gc.ca

New Zealand

Meewwella Building, 4th floor, 329 Galle Road, Colombo 4.
Tel: (011) 255 5995.
nzis@eureka.lk

UK

389 Bauddhaloka Mawatha, Colombo 7.
Tel: (011) 539 0639.
Fax: (011) 539 0694.
Consular.EnquiriesColombo@fco.gov.uk.
www.ukinsrilanka.fco.gov.uk/en

CONVERSION TABLE

FROM	TO	MULTIPLY BY
Inches	Centimetres	2.54
Feet	Metres	0.3048
Yards	Metres	0.9144
Miles	Kilometres	1.6090
Acres	Hectares	0.4047
Gallons	Litres	4.5460
Ounces	Grams	28.35
Pounds	Grams	453.6
Pounds	Kilograms	0.4536
Tons	Tonnes	1.0160

To convert back, for example from centimetres to inches, divide by the number in the third column.

MEN'S SUITS

UK	36	38	40	42	44	46	48
Sri Lanka	46	48	50	52	54	56	58
USA	36	38	40	42	44	46	48

DRESS SIZES

UK	8	10	12	14	16	18
France	36	38	40	42	44	46
Italy	38	40	42	44	46	48
Sri Lanka	34	36	38	40	42	44
USA	6	8	10	12	14	16

MEN'S SHIRTS

UK	14	14.5	15	15.5	16	16.5	17
Sri Lanka	36	37	38	39/40	41	42	43
USA	14	14.5	15	15.5	16	16.5	17

MEN'S SHOES

UK	7	7.5	8.5	9.5	10.5	11
Sri Lanka	41	42	43	44	45	46
USA	8	8.5	9.5	10.5	11.5	12

WOMEN'S SHOES

UK	4.5	5	5.5	6	6.5	7
Sri Lanka	38	38	39	39	40	41
USA	6	6.5	7	7.5	8	8.5

Practical guide

Colombo's imposing Town Hall

USA
210 Galle Road, Kollupitiya, Colombo 3.
Tel: 249 8500.
http://srilanka.usembassy.gov

Emergency telephone numbers
Emergency and Rescue Service *110*
Fire Service *115*
National Help Desk *118*
Police Emergency Service *119*
Police Emergency Service
(from a mobile) *112*

Health
No inoculations or vaccinations are required on entering Sri Lanka unless you have been travelling in an area where yellow fever is prevalent (Africa and parts of South America). However, it is advisable to get vaccinations against diphtheria, tetanus, polio, rabies, hepatitis A and hepatitis B. Malaria tablets do not guarantee immunisation, but reduce the risk significantly. In any case be sure to carry a good mosquito repellent and wear long-sleeved shirts and trousers when mosquitoes are active (around sunset and sunrise). A basic first-aid kit should also contain plasters, calamine lotion to ease the itching from stings, and any antibiotics you may need.

Tap water is not safe to drink, so stick to mineral water and be wary of drinks with ice in rural areas. Likewise, avoid ordering salads in places where hygiene standards seem suspect, to prevent the risk of stomach problems. Many travellers suffer from brief bouts of diarrhoea due to change of climate and diet. It usually clears up by itself, but if it persists, seek medical advice in case you have contracted dysentery. If you plan to spend much time on the beach, use a good sunscreen, wear a hat and keep out of the sun at midday. Unfortunately AIDS is spreading in Sri Lanka due to ignorance about its causes, so either avoid casual sex or use a condom.

If you do need medical attention, visit one of these hospitals:

Apollo Hospital
578 Elvitigala Mawatte, Narahenpita, Colombo 5. Tel: 453 0000.

Colombo General Hospital
10 Regent Street, Colombo 8.
Tel: 269 1111.

Galle General Hospital
Tel: (091) 222 2261.

Kandy General Hospital
Tel: (081) 222 3337.

Negombo General Hospital
Tel: (031) 222 2261.

Insurance

For the sake of peace of mind while on holiday, it makes good sense to take out comprehensive travel insurance with a reputable company. Take a look at the small print before signing, as some policies require you to pay costs upfront and reclaim after, while others will not cover adventure sports such as white-water rafting.

Lost property

There are lost property offices in all airports, railway stations and major bus terminals. If you lose something important like your passport, report it immediately to the tourist police.

Maps

Berndtson & Berndtson produce a detailed Sri Lanka Road Map, while the Nelles Verlag Sri Lanka map includes city maps of Colombo, Kandy, Galle and Anuradhapura. The Sri Lankan Survey Department publishes a decent Road Map of Sri Lanka, as well as a Road Atlas of Sri Lanka that includes some town maps on the back. If you spend much time in Colombo, you may find the A to Z Colombo useful, available in most large bookstores. To browse a wide selection of maps, visit the **Survey Department Map Sales Centre** at 62 Chatham Street, Fort, Colombo, or the **Surveyor General's Office** at Kirula Road, Narahenpita, Colombo. Both are open from 9am–4pm, Mon–Fri.

Media

Surprisingly, there are three national daily newspapers in English – the Daily News, the Daily Mirror (www.dailymirror.lk) and The Island (www.island.lk), as well as three Sunday newspapers – the Sunday Times, Sunday Leader (www.thesundayleader.lk) and Sunday Observer (www.sundayobserver.lk). There are some useful publications specifically for tourists, such as Travelsrilanka (www.travelsrilanka.com) and Explore Sri Lanka, generally distributed in hotels. Magazines like Time and Newsweek are on sale in many hotel bookshops. To get a feel for the predominantly Buddhist perspective of the island, look out for a copy of Buddhist Times.

Several programmes on radio and TV are broadcast in English, and local channels run news broadcasts relayed by Sky, BBC and CNN.

Language

In most tourist centres, you will find plenty of locals who speak English, or at least the delightful Sri Lankan version of the language, so unless you are heading off the beaten track, you will find little need to speak Sinhala or Tamil, the country's two main languages. Nevertheless, as with anywhere in the world, the easiest way to endear yourself to locals is to make an attempt to speak their language. In the following brief list of useful words and phrases, the first translation is Sinhala and the second Tamil.

	Sinhala	Tamil
GENERAL		
Hello	ayubowan	vanakkam
Yes	ou	amam
No	na	illai
Thank you	istuti	nandri
What is your name?	wama mokakda?	ungal peyar yenna?
My name is...	mage nama...	yen peyar...
Excuse me	samavenna	mannikkavum
How much (is this)?	(mika) kiyada?	(idu) yevvalavu?
I don't understand	mata terinneh neh	puriyadu
TRAVELLING		
Where is...?	koheda?	un-ghe?
Left	wama	idatu
Right	dakuna	valatu
Stop	nawathinna	nilungal
Near	lan-ghai	aruhil
Far	durai	tu-rahm
I'd like to hire...	mata... ekak bad-data	enakku... varaykhur vaynu ganna ohna
a car	kar	kaa
a bicycle	baisikel	sai-kul
ACCOMMODATION		
Do you have any rooms available?	kamara tiyanawada?	arekil kidhekkumaa?
How much does the room cost?	kamarayakata gana kiyada?	arayin yenna vilai?
(That is) very expensive	hari ganan	anda vilai mikavum adikur

	Sinhala	**Tamil**
May I see the room please?	kamaraya karnakara penvanna?	tayavu setu arayai parka mudiyama?
Is there hot water?	unuwathura thiyenawada?	kulir satana arai irukkirada?
Is breakfast included?	udeh keh-ematekkada?	kaaleh setrundeen sehrtoh?

TIME AND DAYS

Morning	ude	kalai
Afternoon	dawal	pitpakal
Night	raya	ratri
Now	dang	ippodu
Today	atha	indru
Tomorrow	heta	nalai
Yesterday	iye	netru
Day	dawasa	tinam
Week	sathiya	varum
Month	masey	matam
Monday	Sanduda	Tingal
Tuesday	Angaharuwada	Cevvay
Wednesday	Badada	Putam
Thursday	Brahaspathinda	Viyaran
Friday	Sikurada	Velli
Saturday	Senesurada	Ceni
Sunday	Irida	Nayiri

NUMBERS

One	eka	onru
Two	deka	irandu
Three	tuna	munru
Four	hatara	nangu
Five	paha	aindu
Six	haya	aru
Seven	hata	yeru
Eight	ata	yettu
Nine	namaya	onpadu
Ten	daha	pattu

Money matters

The unit of currency in Sri Lanka is the rupee (Rs), divided into 100 cents. There are coins of 5, 10, 25 and 50 cents, as well as of 1, 2 and 5 rupees. Notes are in denominations of 10, 20, 50, 100, 500, 1,000 and 2,000 rupees. Try to carry as many small-size notes as possible, as it can sometimes be difficult to find change for the Rs500, Rs1,000 and Rs2,000 notes. At the time of writing, £1 was worth approximately Rs165, but you can check out the latest exchange rate at *www.xe.com*

It is easy to exchange all major currencies in the main tourist centres, either in the banks or currency exchange booths, and there is little variation in the rates. Traveller's cheques are also widely accepted, as are major credit cards such as Visa, MasterCard and American Express. There are automatic teller machines (ATMs) in all main towns.

While travelling around, especially on public transport, it's a good idea to keep your cash in a money belt, but as a precaution, keep a couple of big bills in a separate place, so that you are never totally destitute.

Opening hours

Shops generally open from 9am–5pm on Monday to Friday, although many in Colombo stay open until 7pm and shops catering for tourists sometimes stay open until late in the evening. Some shops also open on Saturday mornings, but virtually everywhere is closed on Sundays. Office hours are generally from 8.30am–4.30pm, while bank hours are usually from 9am–3pm. National and local museums open every day except Friday from 9am–5pm, although archaeological museums are open from 8am–5pm daily except Tuesday. All government offices and banks close for public holidays, of which there are many in Sri Lanka (*see 'Public holidays'*).

Police

Hopefully you will not need the services of the police while in Sri Lanka, particularly if you follow a few common-sense rules like not walking on the beach at night or going into very crowded places. When ethnic tensions run high, there are often police checkpoints on main roads around the island. They might ask to see your passport, but more often vehicles carrying tourists are waved straight through. If some misfortune does befall you, contact the Tourist Police in Colombo (*Tel: 243 3747*).

Post offices

Most towns in Sri Lanka have a post office. Opening hours are generally 7am–3pm from Monday to Friday, and many open Saturday morning too. In Colombo, the General Post Office on DR Wijewardene Road in Pettah is open from 7am–6pm from Monday to Saturday. Stamps can also be bought in some large stores.

Be warned, though, that snail mail really earns its name in Sri Lanka, and any postcards you send will probably arrive after you get back home. Post to Europe, for example, takes seven to ten days if you are lucky, much longer if you are not. If you need to send important documents abroad while in Sri Lanka, you should use a courier service such as **DHL** (*Tel: 230 4304*) or **TNT** (*Tel: 230 8444*) in Colombo.

Public holidays

There are lots of public holidays in Sri Lanka, and at these times trains and buses get packed and hotel rates rocket. It is therefore wise to check what holidays will be taking place during your visit so that you can plan accordingly. Despite the congestion and high room rates, it's well worth attending a Sri Lankan festival to appreciate the people's flair for pageantry. The Kandy Perahera (*see p29*), for example, is often dubbed the most spectacular festival in Asia.

Apart from the major festivals listed on *pp28–9*, there are many Hindu, Buddhist, Muslim and Christian festivals throughout the year. The full-moon day each month is celebrated by Buddhists as *poya*, and on these days no alcohol is sold, with the exception of a few tourist enclaves. Most Hindu and Muslim festivals also follow the lunar calendar. To find out exact dates, see *www.srilankatourism.org*

Public transport
By air
Deccan Helicopters operate flights seating 17 passengers from the international airport and from Ratmalana airport near Mount Lavinia to Anuradhapura, Sigiriya, Trincomalee, Minneriya, Koggala and Katurukunda. They also provide helicopter transfer and sightseeing tours to any destination in Sri Lanka. Flying is a good way of saving yourself long journeys by road if you are short of time. Contact **Deccan Aviation**, *The Landmark, 385 Galle Road, Colombo 3. Tel: (011) 237 4500. Fax: (011) 237 0011. www.deccanhelicopters.com*

By bus
Both government and private companies operate bus routes that connect everywhere in the country, and this is certainly a good way to get up close and personal with the locals, as most buses only run when passengers are packed in like sardines. All types of buses can be seen, from rusting and rattling minibuses to sleek, air-conditioned coaches. Prices on the latter are about double those of regular buses, but can be worth it for some extra comfort on a longish journey. Storage space for luggage is minimal, so travel as light as possible. The seats immediately behind the driver are generally reserved for monks. The three main bus stations in Colombo – Central, Saunders Place and Bastian Mawatha – are all located in Pettah district near the train station.

By taxi
Taxis are available throughout the country, although some of them are

in a rather poor condition. A few use meters, but most prefer to negotiate a price before starting. Rates are around Rs30 per kilometre. Radio cabs are available in Colombo (**Quick Radio Cabs**, *Tel: 250 2888*) and Kandy (**Radio Cabs**, *Tel: 223 3322*). To hire a car and driver by the day or week, see companies listed under 'Driving'.

By three-wheeler

Three-wheelers are a novelty for anyone who has not ridden in one before, and they can occasionally be useful in heavy traffic as their small size allows them to squeeze through gaps too narrow for cars. However, they are noisy and expose passengers to clouds of exhaust fumes. Prices must be agreed upon before each journey.

By train

The trains in Sri Lanka don't travel fast, but since distances are not great, no journey lasts too long. There are three different lines that offer the chance to feast your eyes on Sri Lanka's classically tropical scenes. The Coast Line south from Colombo, passing through Hikkaduwa and Galle on the way to Matara, was devastated by the 2004 tsunami but reopened in 2006. The Main Line heads eastwards from Colombo into the hill country, stopping at Kandy and Badulla, a trip that is a treat in itself. The Northern Line heads up to the ancient city of Anuradhapura, then continues to Vavuniya. In Colombo, trains leave from Fort station. There is a helpful Information Office (*Tel: 244 0048*) at the station. There are three classes on Sri Lankan trains, and advance reservations are necessary for first-class travel.

Sustainable tourism

Thomas Cook is a strong advocate of ethical and fairly traded tourism and believes that the travel experience should be as good for the places visited as it is for the people who visit them. That's why we firmly support The Travel Foundation, a charity that develops solutions to help improve and protect holiday destinations, their environment, traditions and culture. To find out what you can do to make a positive difference to the places you travel to and the people who live there, please visit *www.thetravelfoundation.org.uk*

Telephones

To call Sri Lanka from abroad, dial *94*, and then drop the first zero of the area code. Phoning abroad from Sri Lanka is very straightforward, as most hotels have International Direct Dialling (IDD), and there are plenty of public phones that can be operated either by coins or a phone card from newsagents and mini-markets.

Apart from the national phone system, there are several mobile phone companies that offer competitive rates. They are **Mobitel** (*www.mobitellanka. com*), **Dialog GSM** (*www.dialog.lk*),

Celltel (*www.celltelnet.lk*) and
Hutchison Telecom (*www.hutch.lk*).

All numbers are ten digits including
the area code. Area codes are as follows:

Anuradhapura *025*
Colombo *011*
Galle *091*
Jaffna *021*
Kandy *081*
Negombo *031*
Nuwara Eliya *052*
Polonnaruwa *027*
Ratnapura *045*
Sigiriya *066*
Trincomalee *026*
Directory assistance and
    enquiries *1231*

Time

Sri Lanka is 5^1/$_2$ hours ahead of
Greenwich Mean Time (GMT). Thus at
noon in Sri Lanka it is 6.30am in
London (7.30am in British Summer
Time) and 1.30am in New York.

Tipping

Tipping is entirely up to the customer,
but given the extremely low salaries that
most Sri Lankans get, any small offering
will be gratefully accepted. Though
hotels and restaurants add a ten per
cent service charge to the bill, this rarely
finds its way to staff, so if you are happy
with the service you receive, it's a good
idea to leave a few rupees.

Toilets

As you might expect, all top and
mid-range hotels have Western-style
flush toilets, but cheaper places have
squat toilets and provide a bucket
of water in place of toilet paper.
Public toilets are rare and mostly
unappealing.

Tourist information

The Ceylon Tourist Board runs
efficient tourist information centres in
Colombo and Kandy. Their website,
www.srilankatourism.org, is also a
good source of information. Tickets
for the Ancient Cities can be obtained
at the individual sites, or at the
Cultural Triangle Office (*open:
9am–12.30pm & 1.30–4pm daily*),
directly opposite the Tourist
Information Centre in Kandy.

Colombo

Ceylon Tourist Board, *80 Galle Road,
Kollupitiya.*
Tel: 243 7055.

Kandy

Tourist Information Centre,
Palace Square.
Tel: (081) 222 2661.

Travellers with disabilities

There are few concessions to travellers
with disabilities in Sri Lanka. Getting
around by public transport with a
disability is extremely difficult, and
some sites such as Sigiriya might prove
too much of a challenge. However, with
a car and driver many of the country's
attractions are accessible, and the
helpful nature of the locals means
that those with disabilities are well
taken care of.

Practical guide

Index

Acknowledgements

Thomas Cook Publishing wishes to thank CPA MEDIA/DAVID HENLEY for the photographs in this book, to whom the copyright belongs, except for the following images:

DREAMSTIME.COM 1 (Ewen Cameron), 25 (Valery Shanin), 109 (Harald Dilweg), 157 (Emma Holmwood)
CHAAYA HOTELS & RESORTS 175
JULIE CRANE 24
FLICKR/JUNGLE BOY 112
ZEN 152
MOUNT LAVINIA HOTEL 56, 57
PICTURES COLOUR LIBRARY 168
TRANS ASIA HOTEL 173
WORLD PICTURES/PHOTOSHOT 30, 35, 50, 53, 61, 72, 75, 85, 121, 123, 155, 160, 163

For CAMBRIDGE PUBLISHING MANAGEMENT LTD:
Project editor: Karen Beaulah
Typesetter: Donna Pedley
Proofreader: Tom Lee

SEND YOUR THOUGHTS TO BOOKS@THOMASCOOK.COM

We're committed to providing the very best up-to-date information in our travel guides and constantly strive to make them as useful as they can be. You can help us to improve future editions by letting us have your feedback. If you've made a wonderful discovery on your travels that we don't already feature, if you'd like to inform us about recent changes to anything that we do include, or if you simply want to let us know your thoughts about this guidebook and how we can make it even better – we'd love to hear from you.

Send us ideas, discoveries and recommendations today and then look out for your valuable input in the next edition of this title.

Emails to the above address, or letters to Travellers Series Editor, Thomas Cook Publishing, PO Box 227, Coningsby Road, Peterborough PE3 8SB, UK.

Please don't forget to let us know which title your feedback refers to!